Praise for Eric Hansen's

THE BIRD MAN AND THE LAP DANCER

"[There is] sheer lunatic joy to be found in these essays. . . . Hansen's curiosity, ability to meet people on their own terms and willingness to try just about anything make the experience fascinating. His gentle, straightforward prose and the fact that the reader truly never knows what will happen next make *Bird Man* rewarding reading."   —*The Miami Herald*

"[An] inspired collection. . . . These are heartfelt reports from the road, told with simple eloquence and gentle humor."
                                                    —*Seattle Post-Intelligencer*

"Eric Hansen is a traveler's traveler—curious, imaginative, subtle, and brave. *The Bird Man and the Lap Dancer* is the latest report from his life of adventure, told with typical style and verve. It should be read, enjoyed, and passed among friends."
                                            —William Langewiesche, author of
                                American Ground: Unbuilding the World Trade Center

"A riot. . . . Hansen has done things worthy of awe and jealousy."   —*Entertainment Weekly*

"A real travel professional. . . . Hansen draws out-loud guffaws. . . . Unlike many world-wearied writers, Hansen avoids studied cynicism and forced sentimentality."
                                            —*The New York Times Book Review*

"A fine journalist. . . . The way he . . . builds both tension and pathos, is so touching that the reader is drawn into the story. . . . He's so good at descriptions of place, the magic of travel, and the mystery at the edges of the world."

—*The Oregonian*

"In his range, his clarity, and his depth of understanding, Eric Hansen is the match of any travel essayist at work today. To travel well is a rare skill; to write about such travels as well as Hansen does is art." —Joe Kane, author of *Savages*

"Moving. . . . Hansen writes [with] a resonance and psychological depth not usually seen in more routine travel narratives. . . . Each story combines nuanced portraits of memorable characters with lyrical descriptions of human fallibility and generosity . . . [that make] this heartfelt collection a magical and uplifting read." —*The Economist*

"Eric Hansen's lovely book of true-life adventures is a gift. Few writers aspire to such honesty, or manage it so engagingly. A compelling read."

—Bill Barich, author of *Laughing in the Hills*

"Imagine the world of Joseph Conrad invaded by a real-life *Rocky Horror Picture Show*. But there's more to Hansen's stories than mere weirdness and wonder. Some of them are private memories, polished by time; others conceal parables. All are simply and beautifully told."

—Tim Mackintosh-Smith, author of
Yemen: The Unknown Arabia

ERIC HANSEN

THE BIRD MAN AND THE LAP DANCER

Eric Hansen lives in San Francisco, but over the last twenty-five years he has traveled throughout Europe, the Middle East, Australia, Nepal, and Southeast Asia. He is the author of *Stranger in the Forest*, *Motoring with Mohammed*, and *Orchid Fever*. His articles, photographs, and reviews have appeared in *The New York Times*, *National Geographic*, *Travel & Leisure*, *Condé Nast Traveler*, and *Outside* magazine, among other publications worldwide.

He can be reached at ekhansen@ix.netcom.com.

THE
BIRD MAN
AND THE
LAP DANCER

Close Encounters with Strangers

ERIC HANSEN

Vintage Departures
Vintage Books
A Division of Random House, Inc.
New York

FIRST VINTAGE DEPARTURES EDITION, OCTOBER 2005

Copyright © 2004 by Eric Hansen

Lyrics from "The Power Is Mine" are reprinted by kind permission of Lords of Acid.

The Library of Congress has cataloged the Pantheon edition as follows:
Hansen, Eric (Eric K.)
The bird man and the lap dancer :
close encounters with strangers / Eric Hansen.
p. cm.
1. Hansen, Eric (Eric K.)—Travel. 2. Voyages and travels. I. Title.
G465.H354 2004
910.4'1—dc22
2004043433

Vintage ISBN-10: 0-679-77182-4
Vintage ISBN-13: 0-679-77182-1

Author photograph © Dick Sonnen
Book design by Robert C. Olsson

www.vintagebooks.com

Printed in the United States of America
10 9 8 7 6 5 4 3 2

For SMD,
and in memory of my mother
Jeannie C. Hansen, 1923–2001

To season one's destiny with the dust of one's folly, that is the trick.

—Henry Miller

Contents

THE BIRD MAN
AND THE LAP DANCER

ARLETTE AND MADAME PERRUCHE

IT WAS A WARM SUMMER evening when I met Arlette. She was an old woman by then, but in good health. She still wore red lipstick and obviously took pleasure in dressing in a simple but elegant way. Valerie Tatiana von Braunschweig, a former dancer with the Béjart Ballet, and I were driving from Monaco to Juan-les-Pines to spend the summer of 1989. As a way to extend our meandering journey and for me to meet Arlette we decided to take her to dinner at L'Estaminet des Remparts, a small, unpretentious restaurant in Mougins, which is a quaint hilltop village in the south of France. As we settled at our table on the outdoor terrace, Arlette apologized that her companion was too ill to join us. The waiter cleared away the fourth place setting and returned with a bottle of chilled rosé. He poured the glasses and set the bottle on the table as Arlette began the story of how she met Madame Perruche.

For nearly forty years, Arlette had lived in a modestly furnished apartment in the hills behind Cannes. She was once a principal dancer for the Marquis de Cuevas and the Ballet Russe of Monte Carlo, where she had danced with Valerie's

mother fifty years earlier. But when the company failed Arlette was too old to join another company. And so she became
a teacher at a local ballet school which catered to well-to-do
families with young daughters of average talent. She lived in
reduced circumstances as the Cannes of her youth succumbed
to the traffic and featureless concrete monoliths that began to
dominate the older hillside neighborhoods of summer homes
covered in blooms of ancient bougainvillea. But she lived fru-
gally and managed to get by on a modest salary from the ballet school. Arlette drove an ancient motor scooter and on most
mornings she went to a small park near the train station to
feed the stray cats.

There was a street woman who frequented the same park.
She was known as Madame Perruche (Madame Parakeet).
The woman was given her name because she fed the birds, but
also because of her frail body and hooked nose. She owned
two sweaters. One blue and one black, to go with her blue
skirt with the white polka dots. No one knew much about the
woman or where she came from. She slept on a park bench
and used *poste restante* at the main post office to receive mail.
No one could remember when she first appeared in the neighborhood, but it had been years ago and by the time Arlette met
the woman Madame Perruche was more or less accepted as a
permanent fixture in the park.

Arlette usually smiled or said hello to the woman during
her visits to the park, but Madame Perruche rarely replied and
when she did it was with a vigorous shake of her head or a
brusque huffing sound. Her years on the street had made her
wary of strangers and it was clear that she wanted as little
contact with people as possible. She preferred the company of

birds. Several mornings each week Madame Perruche could be found seated on the same park bench. Birds would flutter around eating seed and dried bread at her feet and occasionally one would perch on her hand for a brief conversation. Wild birds would take sunflower seeds from her lips.

Then one autumn day, as she was feeding the cats, Arlette thought about how odd it was that most people felt uncomfortable about giving food to humans but not to animals. Arlette brought the woman a fresh baguette and a small wedge of cheese.

"Merci, madame," said Madame Perruche sharply, as she snatched the food from her hand and walked away.

The following week Arlette persuaded the woman to go to a local café for a cup of coffee and a pastry. The regular patrons, hunched over the zinc bar sipping their midmorning pastis, appeared to take scant notice of the women. But as soon as the women were out the door, there must have been words, because their cruel comments were later passed on to Arlette by her grocer. Arlette's friends, knowing her generous habits, urged her not to get involved with a woman who lived on the streets.

When winter set in that year the mistral blew from the north bringing days of bitterly cold, rainy weather. Sitting at her breakfast table, sipping a steamy cup of tea and listening to the torrent of raindrops pounding on the windowpanes, Arlette could not bear the thought of the old woman wandering the streets looking for shelter. And so, during a lull in the storm, Arlette drove to the park and returned home with Madame Perruche, and her plastic bags of belongings, perched on the back of the motor scooter.

"She was soaking wet when I found her," Arlette told us. "I gave her a dressing gown and a bath towel, and left her with a cup of *chocolat chaud* while I took her clothes to the laundromat."

Madame Perruche stayed for two days until the weather warmed and then she returned to her park bench and her birds. Arlette's friends were horrified when they heard that she had allowed a person from the street to sleep in her home.

"But what are you thinking!?" a neighbor yelled at Arlette once Madame Perruche had left.

The two women continued to get to know each other in the little park, and, when Arlette was invited to visit friends in Paris, she asked Madame Perruche if she would like to stay in the apartment and take care of the plants and collect the mail. Arlette's friends threw up their hands in exasperation when they heard that she was planning to loan her apartment to the bird woman.

"Impossible! There won't be a thing left when you get back," they warned her. "She will make a copy of your key. You won't be able to get rid of her."

Arlette didn't listen to the advice of her friends, but to avoid problems with the doorman and the other tenants in her apartment building Arlette gave Madame Perruche a new pair of espadrilles and some clothes from her closet that she no longer wore. She installed Madame Perruche in her apartment, with a small sum of money for groceries, and then packed her bag and left for Paris.

"But weren't you concerned about your belongings?" I asked Arlette as she paused to take a bite of her dinner.

"The only thing of value that I own is a photo album from

my youth. And what sort of person would steal something like that?" She laughed.

According to the neighbors, Madame Perruche rarely left the apartment while Arlette was in Paris. By the time Arlette returned a week later she found her home in an astonishing state. The woman had cleaned the entire apartment, washed and ironed the bed linen, scrubbed and waxed the floors, and cleaned the windows inside and out. Fresh flowers, picked from the park, were set in a small vase on the kitchen table. Arlette was delighted with what she saw, and suggested that Madame Perruche stay. She could take the small room off the kitchen. The bird woman accepted, but only on the condition that she could make herself useful. She continued to clean the house and helped with the shopping and cooking.

Arlette had the good sense not to pry into the woman's life, and each morning they continued to walk to the square to feed the cats and birds. Madame Perruche never talked about her past, but there were telltale signs in her behavior that convinced Arlette that the woman had come from a good family. She took note of how the woman set the table and folded the bottom corners of a bedsheet; and how she paused to listen to Beethoven's Violin Sonata No. 6 in A Major that Arlette played on the phonograph one afternoon. The two women lived simply and quietly, but many of Arlette's friends found it impossible to accept this new living arrangement without comment. They thought Arlette had lost her mind. Several neighbors suspected the women were lovers. Arlette told us these possibilities were perfectly in keeping with their small minds and empty lives.

The first winter passed and early in the spring a letter

arrived at *poste restante* for Madame Perruche. The return
address was of a law firm in Lyon. Madame Perruche left the
letter unopened on the breakfast table for a week, but Arlette
finally encouraged her to read the contents. The letter was
brief. Madame Perruche was requested to contact the law firm
as soon as possible. A distant relative had died and Madame
Perruche had inherited an unspecified amount of money.

"Maybe it is a great sum," Arlette suggested, urging the
woman to reply at once.

Madame Perruche didn't want any contact with her past,
but after two weeks of putting it off, she let Arlette convince
her to write back. Within days of her reply a telegram arrived
with the startling news that she had indeed inherited a great
sum of money. The lawyer arranged for papers to be signed
and notarized, a new bank account was opened in Cannes,
funds were transferred, and within two months Madame Perruche found herself with a small fortune.

Uncertain of what to do, she continued living with
Arlette. She kept herself busy cleaning the apartment, but she
immediately insisted on sharing the rent and other expenses.

"You can imagine how quickly the news of this inheri-
tance cooled the hysteria of the neighbors." Arlette laughed.
The waiter set a generous slice of fig tart and an expresso in
front of Arlette as she continued her story. "The neighbors,
those meddlesome, bourgeois fools. They had nothing better
to occupy their time than to talk about us," she said.

As summer arrived Madame Perruche announced that she
would like to buy an apartment. She invited Arlette to move in
with her, but Arlette, who had always helped others, found it
very difficult to accept favors. She had grown accustomed to

giving rather than receiving, but in time the woman convinced Arlette that she was merely trying to return a favor and that there was no reason why her sudden good fortune should break up their friendship.

A real estate agent found a more beautiful and larger apartment not far from the park where the two women had first met. Madame Perruche paid cash and by the end of the summer they had painted the rooms and moved in. Arlette brought her photo album, her motor scooter, furniture, bedding, pots, pans, dishes and kitchen utensils, and she insisted on paying a modest rent.

"As you please," said Madame Perruche.

At the first sign of winter Madame Perruche suggested that the two of them take a journey. Arlette explained that she could not afford to travel, but that she would be happy to stay behind and take care of the apartment. Madame Perruche laughed at this suggestion and returned later that day with two one-way boat tickets from Marseilles to Alexandria.

"It will be warmer there," she explained over Arlette's protests. And so, with little knowledge of their destination, no hotel reservations and no tour arrangements, the two women bravely set forth to discover Egypt. They visited the sights of Cairo, then sailed up the Nile on a converted felucca, and explored Luxor and the Valley of the Kings. They saw such things as mummified baboons and crocodiles.

Toward the end of dinner, Arlette reached into her bag to show us pictures from her photo album. In one photo, the two of them were standing in front of the great temple at Karnak. In a second photo, Madame Perruche was perched on a camel in front of the pyramids. She had a pair of sunglasses set on her nose and a wide-brimmed straw sun hat tied at the chin with black ribbon. The photos had been taken ten years earlier.

After dinner, we drove Arlette home. That was the last time I saw her. She no longer sends me postcards from places like Fez, Prague or Madrid, but common friends keep me informed. According to them, most of Arlette's acquaintances in Cannes have either moved away or died or lost their minds. Arlette still manages to ride her motor scooter to the weekly open-air market when the weather is fine. She no longer pays rent and now that both she and Madame Perruche are getting frail, a woman comes by the apartment once a week to vacuum, and do the laundry, and to prepare a few simple meals. They still try to get away for a trip during the winter, but in recent years they have seldom ventured any further than Paris.

Spring is their favorite season to be at home. It is a beautiful time in the south of France. The migratory birds are returning from North Africa and mimosa trees grace the boulevards with their fragrant bright yellow blooms. Most mornings, at that time of year, the two friends can be found in a small park near the train station. Children run by the park on their way to school, but they hardly notice the two old ladies standing at opposite ends of the square where one is feeding the cats, and the other is feeding the birds.

LIFE AT THE GRAND HOTEL

AN ORANGE MORNING LIGHT filtered into my room as an outboard motor coughed to life somewhere in the distance. The French doors that opened onto the second-floor verandah allowed a sea breeze to billow the curtains at the doorway and fill the room with a heady fragrance of frangipani flowers. Sections of corrugated-metal roofing began to creak and groan as they warmed in the sun and there was the far-off sound of a teakettle whistling. The Grand Hotel was coming to life.

Pushing the mosquito net aside, I wrapped a towel around my waist and walked to the verandah railing to scan the waterfront. The hundred-year-old weathered floorboards felt dry and smooth beneath my feet. Little zebra finches flitted along the eaves and white cockatoos screeched at one another as they flew between the coconut palms. It was a familiar scene.

Twenty years earlier I had worked at the hotel, and most mornings I stood at this same spot to take in the wide view of scattered white clouds as their shadows drifted over a turquoise sea. The scene evoked sensations and memories that beckoned from a previous life that has never quite settled in my mind. Dressed in my towel, I strolled along the verandah, took in the warm sea air and thought about the circumstances that originally brought me to Thursday Island and the Grand Hotel.

In those days I was a cook and deckhand on the *Cape Bedford,* an eighty-five-foot-long steel-hulled prawn trawler that worked the north coast of Australia. I operated a massive wire-rope drum winch that controlled the starboard-side prawn net. When I wasn't on deck, I worked in the galley, baking bread and cinnamon rolls, shelling prawns, filleting fish, peeling potatoes and preparing three meals a day for the crew of five. I baked cookies, gingerbread and banana bread for the night watch, when one of the crew, in rotation, would take a three-hour shift to keep the boat on course while the rest slept. I chose the three A.M. to six A.M. watch so that I could set the autopilot and then sit on the foredeck with a cup of hot tea and watch the star-filled night sky followed by the sunrise.

We fished the bays and estuaries of Melville and Bathurst Islands, the Cobourg Peninsula, Croker Island, and the entire Arnhem Land coast as far east as Blue Mud Bay and Groote Eylandt in the Gulf of Carpentaria. We refueled at remote mining camps and Aboriginal mission stations with names like Maningrida, Milingimbi, and Alyangula. Occasionally we anchored the trawler and rowed the dinghy ashore to spear huge mud crabs in the mangroves. At the time, I was oblivious to the fact that twenty-foot-long man-eating saltwater crocodiles shared the same habitat.

On one of our trips ashore we shot a young water buffalo.

We butchered it on deck and then called all the nearby boats to a small, unnamed and uninhabited island for a raucous barbecue and bonfire on the beach that lasted until dawn. After six months on the boat I could navigate by the stars, mend shark holes in the nets, splice rope in the dark, stitch my own flesh without anesthetic and take part in the time-honored tradition of drunken barroom brawls that frequently broke out whenever the crew went ashore.

We spent weeks, sometimes months at sea, following a routine that varied little from day to day. To keep the boat and the trawling nets in working order, we rarely slept for more than three or four hours at a time. We put out our nets, read books or napped on deck, hauled in the catch, hoisted it overhead and then untied the bottoms of the nets and dumped the catch onto the waist-high sorting tables. We regularly caught green turtles and venomous sea snakes. If the turtles were gasping for air we set them aside until they recovered before dropping them overboard unharmed. Occasionally, three- to five-foot-long bills from sawtooth sharks would show up in the nets. We saved these tooth-studded souvenirs to sell on shore. The prawns were raked into flat, waxed cardboard boxes that we topped up with water and then stowed in the huge walk-in freezer below deck. The trawler could hold more than 90,000 pounds of frozen prawns, most of which went to the Japanese market. We lived on prawns, reef fish, scallops, a flat lobster-like creature known as a Moreton Bay Bug (*Thenus orientalis*), pasta, rice, eggs, fresh bread, jam, cabbage, tea, frozen chicken, and tinned baked beans.

One day a thrashing fourteen-foot-long hammerhead shark dropped out of a net and onto the sorting table. I slung a noose around its tail and we hauled it up into the rigging with a plan to drop it overboard. But the shark wrapped itself up in all of the overhead ropes and we couldn't get it down. It was too big and too dangerous to cut free while still alive and so the skipper blew its brains out with a rifle. Standing aft, I was splattered with flying flecks of cartilage, flesh and clots of gore. The exit wound in the shark's head was the size of a tea saucer. Then we climbed into the rigging to unravel the knotted ropes before winching the huge, inert body over the side. The sea exploded in a feeding frenzy by the school of scavenging sharks. Seagulls dropped from the air to dive for morsels at the edge of the churning patch of sea. Minutes later, the surface of the water was calm with no trace of the feeding sharks or their meal. Whenever I climbed up into the rigging I could see dozens of huge, dark, ominous shapes trailing in our wake. By night, the powerful lights on our outriggers illuminated smaller sharks four to six feet long. Large and small, they followed the fishing boat, waiting to attack and eat anything that fell overboard.

Just before Christmas, 1974, we were working the sandy flats of Shark Bay on the north coast of Melville Island when we heard the first radio reports of a cyclone forming somewhere to our north in the Arafura Sea. Our original plan had been to arrive in Darwin for Christmas Eve, but as the weather reports started describing a severe tropical storm moving southwest at 6 knots with winds of 140 kms per hour just north of Melville Island we canceled Christmas, pulled in our nets, prepared the trawler for heavy weather, and headed east through building seas and torrential rain. By that time the cyclone had a name: Tracy.

The day before Christmas Cyclone Tracy veered south around Cape Fourcroy at the western tip of Bathurst Island, and then abruptly changed course and headed east-southeast toward Darwin. Like most of the big trawlers in the fleet, when we heard the cyclone warnings we headed far out to sea to ride out the storm. Late that night, near Cape Don at the tip of the Cobourg Peninsula, we were hit by the edge of the cyclone. I will never forget the high-pitched screaming of the wind as our boat plowed through the heavy seas, pitching and rolling, decks awash, lifeboat and supplies lashed to the rear deck, and the entire crew standing by in the wheelhouse listening to the radio; and much later, with duffel bags packed with personal belongings, we just waited to do what was needed to save the ship or abandon it. Cyclone Tracy hit Darwin around midnight. Six hours later, according to early radio reports coming in from Singapore the next morning, the city had ceased to exist.

Other prawn trawlers in the fleet went down that night and a few of their last calls, reporting increasing wind speeds, deteriorating sea conditions, and engine and pump failure, came through on the crackling marine band radio. There was nothing to do but listen, report our position and maintain control of the trawler. Sixteen people died at sea that night, most of them trying to save their vessels. One of them was a Japanese friend who drowned when his battered trawler sank at the height of the cyclone while tied to the Stokes Hill wharf in Darwin.

We couldn't return to Darwin because of the cyclone damage and the state of emergency. Winds had gusted up to 250 kms an hour and 90 percent of the town was destroyed.

Thirty-five thousand residents were being evacuated, and I had no idea of the fate of my friends who lived in Darwin. But our trawler had survived the storm and I felt like I had been given another life. I was twenty-six years old. It was near the end of the fishing season, so we stored our nets and fishing gear and headed for our home port Cairns on the Queensland coast to unload our catch. But first we would have to refuel at a place called Thursday Island. The trawler moved east across the Gulf of Carpentaria and five days later we entered the Torres Strait that separates the tip of Cape York Peninsula from the southern coast of New Guinea.

Three of us stood on deck that night peering into a wall of mist as the trawler eased its way through a blood-warm sea. Water lapped the hull and the air was heavy with the smell of the nearby islands. Our radar indicated we were within one hundred yards of Thursday Island but we were lost, as our searchlight continued its feeble sweep through the darkness. Standing still, I held my breath to listen for the sound of the shore break. Sometime later the bow lookout caught sight of a dock and called out the direction to the skipper. The engines reversed, then surged as we glided to a stop alongside the fuel dock. A black man stepped from the shadows. Without a word he took the bow and stern lines, threw them over the rusted cleats then moved off into the night. It was a bad place to tie up. The dock was exposed to the weather and the splintered decking swayed noisily in the strong current. A wind blew from the south and there was the smell of sump oil and rotten pilings. We put out our tire bumpers and set springer lines to help stabilize the trawler against the changing tide. We would have to wait until the morning to take on fuel and water.

Once ashore, the crew followed the late-night sounds of music and loud voices. After Cyclone Tracy and the long fishing season, we were ready for some life-embracing activities; and, as I soon discovered, there were few places on earth better suited to this purpose than the public bar of the Grand Hotel.

The place was packed, but we managed to find an empty space at the end of the bar. The smell of stale beer, cigarette smoke, dust, sump oil, honest sweat and dried vomit was kept in circulation by the slow-moving blades of overhead fans. Broken chairs were roughly piled in a corner and shards of glass and busted-up window frames lay strewn along the baseboard. The debris, we learned from the tattooed island woman who brought us our tins of QT Lager, was the result of a bingo game that had gone out of control the previous night. Three men were in the hospital and Friday night bingo was suspended indefinitely. The woman proudly pointed out her black eye from bingo night and laughed as she went back to tending the other customers.

Seated next to me was a young islander. He was pear-shaped, about six foot four, and weighed at least 275 pounds. He introduced himself as Billy. He had the largest pair of fists I had ever seen and he looked like the sort of man who knew how to use them.

"HEY! What do ya think ah me new watch?" Billy asked. He held out his wrist to show me a stainless steel watch. His forearm was about the size of my thigh.

"Nice one," I said, taking a sip of beer.

"Yeah? Ya like it, do ya? Well I'll fight ya for it then."
Billy said. He unfastened the steel band and slapped the watch
on the bar top. I tried to convince my new friend that I didn't
need a watch, but Billy was too far gone for such tactics.

"What? Ya don' like me watch? Ain't it goodenuff for
you, ya white mothafuckah? COME ON!" he said, holding up
his fists. I had been in the bar for about three minutes. As if on
cue, several nearby people stepped back to clear a space for us.
I bought Billy a beer, to buy some time. Then I leaned forward and told him in a quiet voice that, just between the two
of us, I didn't want to fight because I was concerned he might
slip in my blood and hurt himself. He liked that and Billy soon
forgot about beating me to a pulp. Instead, he erupted in a
spasm of belly laughs, slipped his watch back onto his wrist,
and pounded me on the back in a friendly sort of way. Then
he told me to buy him another beer.

No sooner had I pacified Billy than I looked down the bar
and made eye contact with another big islander. Instinctively,
the man held up his fists and started shadow boxing. I looked
around to see who he might be picking a fight with. It could
only be Billy or me, and I was pretty sure it wasn't Billy.

"Ignore that wanker . . . ," said Billy, waving the man off.

We fell into conversation about the Torres Strait Islands
and people who lived there. Billy taught me my first local
phrase. In addition to English, both Eastern Language (known
as Meriam) and Western Language are spoken but regardless of one's language, anyone who has spent more than a
few days on Thursday Island knows the expression "Kubalah
wah?" Politely translated, it means "Would you like to have
sex?" In response to this question there are only two possible

answers and both of them are "yes." The first means "Yes, I would like to"—and the second means "Yes, but not with you. You are not man (or woman) enough to please me." A favorite sport among the men, Billy told me, was to sleep (at different times) with the daughter, her mother and her grandmother. This feat was known as the Grand Slam, and according to several men and women at the bar it was a common activity enjoyed by all participants. They talked about the Grand Slam in the way some people discuss golf.

Billy was becoming increasingly more incoherent and unpredictable, so I decided to take a stroll around the ground floor of the hotel. In a room adjoining the bar I came upon a stocky, three-hundred-pound man in his mid-fifties who was climbing onto the pool table. Dressed in a blue singlet and a pair of faded shorts, he appeared to be in a trance as he stood barefoot on the edge of the table. His arms were stretched out in front of his chest as if he was preparing to dive into a small swimming pool of green felt. A game was in progress, but the players and spectators in the crowded room acted as if the man was nothing more than a block of cue chalk resting on the cushion. Without warning, the big man crouched down like a springboard diver, then suddenly launched himself into the air backward. He brought up his knees into a neat tuck and completed a perfect backflip, landing catlike on the wooden floor. No one responded to this extraordinary feat, and I soon discovered why. They had all seen this trick before . . . and it was merely a prelude to what was to come as the regular patrons started warming up for the evening's entertainment.

I placed some money on the pool table and when it was my

turn to play I was introduced to the Thursday Island handshake. The T.I. handshake, as it is commonly referred to
throughout the Northern Territory and Queensland, is a traditional form of greeting practiced by young, and sometimes
not so young island women. The "handshake," when properly executed, takes place when a stranger, dressed ideally in
loose shorts without underpants, is momentarily distracted.
At that precise moment the woman reaches up the man's
shorts and gives his penis a friendly tug. As I leaned forward
to rack the balls on the pool table, I received my first Thursday Island handshake. It came from Olive Nona—the beautiful barmaid and, as I later learned, the reigning women's
fist-fighting champion of the Grand Hotel. Olive walked
slowly back to the bar. She acknowledged the catcalls from
her friends and then briefly looked back at me over her shoulder with half-closed eyes and a slight lifting motion of her
chin.

Getting back to the first night's entertainment—the next
performance was by Gene Cox, an American cowboy from
Florida who operated the cattle lease on nearby Prince of
Wales Island. He executed intricate lariat tricks and sang
Gene Autry songs while I fell into conversation with Goggle-
eyed Tammy, the sixty-three-year-old, one-eyed good-time
girl, and her friend Ralph Nona, better known as Big Black
Ralph, skipper of the pearling lugger *Ruby Scarlet*. That night
I also met Lighthouse Lenny, the man who maintained the
unmanned lighthouses up and down the Great Barrier Reef,
Captain Wheatfever—who I suspect had never set foot on a
boat of any sort—and a man they called Screaming Eagle.
With the passage of time, it is difficult to pinpoint the high-

light of that evening, but I would guess it was probably the sight of a man spitting his flaming dentures off the end of the wharf, as he tried to teach me how to blow fireballs with a mouthful of kerosene and a burning newspaper.

The Grand Hotel had a dreamlike, otherworldly feel to it. The bar was a paradise of strangers and judging from the bawdy, carnival-like activity that took place the first night I recognized a rare opportunity. Seldom does one have the chance to enjoy the company of people who have so completely given themselves over to the cultivation of the low life in such style and with such gusto. They had elevated this sort of behavior to an art form and I wanted to be part of it. I don't know if I was suffering some sort of traumatic disorder from Cyclone Tracy, or if all those months at sea had destroyed my judgment and sense of self-preservation. I simply told myself that the prawn season was over for the year and there was no reason for me to remain on the trawler with the rest of the crew. My mind was brimming with thoughts about serendipity, fate and good fortune while the expressions on the faces of my gap-toothed, tattooed shipmates clearly conveyed their concerns about my feeble mental state.

"Have you gone crackers?" asked the skipper, when he learned of my intentions to stay on the island.

At the bar, I asked around for accommodation. There were two choices: the reasonably priced Florie Kennedy's Boarding House or the Grand Hotel. The Grand seemed like a tough, ramshackle sort of place, but after Olive Nona, the barmaid, told me about Florie Kennedy's Miracle Mile I reconsidered my options. The Miracle Mile was the stretch of road that lay between the front door of the Grand Hotel and

Florie Kennedy's Boarding House. According to Olive, the road was so named because if you didn't get robbed, beaten, raped, murdered, seduced or lost on the way back to Florie Kennedy's after a night at the Grand Hotel it was a miracle. Seated next to me at the bar, an older Aboriginal man by the name of Wally Green Ant leaned forward to share some local knowledge with me.

"Hey . . . lemme tell you . . . you whitefella. You walk down the road there in da nighttime and maybe two thing gonna happen to you. Either you gonna find trouble-trouble . . . or trouble-trouble gonna find you."

After hearing this, I decided on the more centrally located Grand Hotel.

I found Keith, the manager of the hotel, and asked him about the possibility of working for room and board. By the look of things he could use some help repairing the public bar and the rest of the hotel. I had a set of carpenter's tools on the boat and we soon made a deal. In exchange for working from eight A.M. until noon each day he would provide me with a bedroom and two meals a day plus $100 per week. It seemed like a fair arrangement. I collected my duffel bag and toolbox from the boat, bid farewell to my disbelieving shipmates, and moved into the Grand Hotel that night.

My room on the second floor was furnished with a table that had two and a half legs, a wooden chair that lay on the floor in pieces, a cardboard box for a bedside table and a stained, lumpy mattress that lay upon the rusted wire mesh of a hammocklike bed. An overhead fan and a fly-specked bare bulb of low wattage hung from the center of the ceiling. Empty beer cans, peanut shells, tabloid newspapers, paint flakes from the ceiling and cigarette butts covered the wood floor. The door was missing. Inspecting the room, I couldn't help but wonder what the meals would be like.

The following morning I found a door for my room and then spent several hours sweeping, scrubbing and mopping the floor. I washed the windows, repaired the furniture and made my room habitable. For the next several months I worked at the Grand Hotel as the maintenance carpenter. My job was to get up each morning and repair the damage caused the previous night by the patrons of the public bar. With the shattered windows, doors wrenched off their hinges, vandalized toilet stalls, and miscellaneous damage from fistfights and late-night break-ins I often found myself hard-pressed to have the place in reasonable order each day before the next onslaught began at noontime.

I solved the nightly toilet-stall door destruction problem by hanging the door on a triple set of hinges that I fastened through the wall with twelve-inch-long stainless steel bolts. The sink and urinal were demolished with a bowling ball one night. This came as a surprise because I was unaware of any bowling alley on the island. The vandalism never stopped completely, but it eventually began to taper off at about the same rate I started making friends with the regular patrons.

Surrounded by boisterous, violent, degenerate and wildly unpredictable characters, I found life at the Grand Hotel unnerving and irresistible. One night a woman by the name of Big Mary went toe-to-toe with another woman. The two of them started slapping each other and throwing punches, but soon they ripped off each other's blouses and ended up barebreasted rolling on the floor biting, kicking, punching and scratching. Shredded bits of blouse, tufts of hair, and blood spots marked their progress as they fought their way from the public bar to the poolroom, to the verandah, and then back to the bar over the course of the ten-minute combat. During this time raucous laughter and words of encouragement were offered, and no one lifted a finger to stop the floor show.

But life at the Grand Hotel wasn't all about being drunk and disorderly. There was another side to Thursday Island which slowly began to reveal itself. Old pearl-shell divers came to the bar to tell me their stories. A ham radio operator put me in contact with friends who had been evacuated from Darwin to Sydney, and then Ralph Nona invited me to Badu Island. Strictly speaking, I was not allowed to travel to the outer islands without permission from the Department of Aboriginal Affairs. When I mentioned this to Ralph, he told me bluntly: "That office it full of whitefellas. These our islands, so you got permission. You understand?"

On the trip to Badu we traveled on Ralph's pearling lugger *Ruby Scarlet*, and during the journey I didn't once see a chart or a compass as he negotiated the confusion of tides, back eddies, crosscurrents and coral reefs. Someone must have seen me depart on the *Ruby Scarlet*, because by the time we arrived at Badu, the Department of Aboriginal Affairs had already sent a radio message explaining I was en route and that I did not have a permit to visit the island. The islanders were instructed to lock me up and send me back to Thursday Island on the first available boat. Ralph's uncle, Chief Tamoy Nona, spoke solemnly to the small welcoming party that had gathered on the beach. With Ralph translating, Tamoy conveyed the following message:

"You have come to our island illegally and it is my responsibility to take you into custody. It is my duty to send you back tomorrow morning. But unfortunately for the Department of Aboriginal Affairs that will not be possible. Tonight we are beginning a village celebration. No boats are going back to Thursday Island until after the party. And judging from last year's party, that should be in about three days' time. As chief of the island I order you to stay with us and enjoy yourself. Welcome to Badu Island."

Everyone broke out in laughter and Ralph took me home to stay with his family. For the next three days and nights I ate barbecued dugong blubber, drank warm gin out of bottles and watched huge men dressed in lengths of red fabric known as lava-lavas as they danced in front of a crackling bonfire. A group of tribesmen from Papua New Guinea painted themselves up and danced for nearly an hour without rest. The first night on Badu Island I was introduced to Lily, the niece of Chief Tamoy Nona. She made eyes at me. I smiled back to be polite, but she seemed a bit young and I found the wide gap between her two front teeth to be disconcerting. Not my type. Over the course of the evening, however, as the festivities heated up and the drinking and dancing continued, I started to exchange brief glances with Lily. Strangely enough, the more I looked at her the smaller the gap in her teeth became. I'm not sure if this was due to the dugong blubber or the gin, but by three A.M., the gap in her teeth was hardly noticeable when she invited me into an empty bedroom. We kissed and laughed and wrestled on the bed fully dressed for a short while, but apart from some harmless groping nothing much happened and I soon went back to the fire where I sat next to Charlie

Nona, Ralph's brother. Charlie had a huge stomach, and when he laughed, which was often, his entire body shook like a big happy pudding. Perspiration flowed down his face onto the folds of his chocolate-brown stomach.

"TOO MUCH HAPPY!" he cried out, elbowing me in the ribs as he passed the bottle of gin. "Whitefella, him too much happy! NOW DRINK!!!" he commanded.

I drank, ate more dugong and generally had a fine time.

True to their word, the islanders kept me in custody for the next three days. The hospitality was so formidable that it was quite impossible to walk past a house without being invited in for something to eat or drink. I managed a few brief naps, but each evening the drinking and dancing continued until dawn the next day. By the third morning I was ready to go. As promised to the Department of Aboriginal Affairs, Chief Tamoy Nona sent me back to Thursday Island on the first available boat. Totally exhausted, I fell asleep on deck and remember nothing of the return voyage apart from the gentle vibration of the engine, the warm salt-sea air and the shifting sunlight.

For the next two months that I lived in the Torres Strait, I continued to work at the Grand Hotel and I made frequent extended trips to the outer islands. I visited a nearby island that had a church with a leaded-glass window constructed entirely of broken beer and liquor bottles. One night at the bar of the Grand Hotel I was asked to caretake a cattle station on Prince of Wales Island, which lay to the southwest of Thursday Island. The owner, Gene Cox, was the cowboy from Florida who had performed the lariat tricks in the poolroom the night I arrived on the prawn trawler. He wanted to go to Brisbane for a month to visit his family and he needed someone to look after his house and livestock. I hardly knew the man, but he didn't hesitate entrusting me with everything he owned. Apart from a small camp of Aborigines on a beach to the north, I would be the sole inhabitant of the island. Just before sunset on the day Gene showed me around his property, we came upon an old stock horse lying on the ground. The animal was dying, but rather than go for his gun Gene stayed with the horse, talking quietly and stroking its neck until it died shortly before dawn the following day. Gene was an unsentimental character, and given the inhospitable land and harsh climate I was surprised by the obvious love he felt for his animals.

The one-room homestead lay at the end of a winding river lined with mangrove trees, and when the tides were high I could cross the shallow reef at the mouth of the river, using Gene's eighteen-foot-long aluminum dinghy, and reach the main wharf on Thursday Island in an hour. I also had the use of an old tractor to bring food and supplies from an upriver dock to the house. But apart from painting the house, shooting wild dogs and looking out for stray cattle there wasn't much to do, so I spent most of my time exploring the island. I couldn't imagine myself shooting a dog until the day I was walking through a eucalyptus forest looking for a horse that had wandered off with its hobbles still attached. In among the trees I found two dead calves with their necks and ears chewed away. Black flies filled the eye sockets and swarmed over the entrails where wild pigs had eaten into the stomach cavity.

After that, I never wandered far from the house without the rifle. It was a vintage, lever-action Winchester Model 94. I shot the dogs on sight and left them for the pigs.

The solitude I found on Prince of Wales Island balanced nicely the boisterous and unpredictable company in the Grand Hotel. Once a week I took the boat to Thursday Island to buy groceries and visit with friends, and it was during this time that I realized the islands were changing me in unexpected ways. By spontaneously leaving the fishing trawler and surrendering to the mood of the place I was meeting people and finding myself in situations that I could never have imagined months earlier. This revelation made me completely lose my appetite for making plans.

One morning I loaded the boat with a blanket, some food, and a "billycan" for making tea. Slowly heading south along the west coast of the island, I traveled as far as a remote beach where a wooded canyon opened onto the sea. After unloading the boat on the beach, I found a safe anchorage and swam ashore to set up camp. I smelled smoke late in the afternoon, but it was not until well after nightfall that I saw the first lick of red flames far up the valley. A bush fire was burning in my direction. The warm evening wind soon fanned the flames into a proper fire that began to burn its way down the valley. Flames shot up the tree trunks, fed by the tangle of dry vines, before exploding through the tree crowns in spectacular fireballs that filled the air with showers of sparks. The wall of fire started to move toward me at a swift rate, but I felt secure on the beach where there was nothing to burn. Overcome by some primitive urge, I took off my clothes hoping to soon feel the radiant heat of the fire against my skin. I figured that if the fire became too intense I could always wade into the water. Unfortunately, that plan was formed before I noticed the large fins moving up and down the shallows just off the beach. The scene was illuminated by a fantastic orange glow interspersed with bright flashes of light as dried pandanus palms burst into flame less than a hundred feet from where I stood. As the flames reached the top of the beach they ignited a row of dead bushes so that I was driven by the heat into knee-deep water.

Mesmerized by the spectacle, I was suddenly engulfed by a wall of frantic insects that swept across the beach just ahead of the flames. It was at that moment that I heard something large swishing through the water just behind me. Turning around in alarm, I suddenly realized that sharks were feeding on fish that had been attracted by the light of the fire. I leapt forward to the water's edge where I crouched naked on the wet sand trying to avoid the heat of the flames. It was rapidly becoming unbearably hot, and then suddenly the flames vanished. With nothing left to burn the fire extinguished itself a mere thirty feet from where I huddled. Choking on a throat full of insects, I was left in darkness with my skin tingling from the heat. The valley fell quiet and I walked into the burned areas sniffing the air like an animal. The ground was hot beneath my bare feet, but not unbearably so. That night I strung my mosquito net from a smoldering tree branch and slept on a blanket on the warm earth. Embers continued to flare up in patches throughout the night, but when I left at dawn all that remained of the fire were a few plumes of smoke drifting across the blackened valley.

Further down the coast, I tied up the boat at the bank of a small tributary stream and hiked inland to check a rocky outcrop for signs of aboriginal dreamtime paintings. As I paused in an open grassland to get my bearings I happened to glance at my feet. About eighteen inches from where I stood I saw a gold wristwatch with a broken leather strap lying on the ground. I picked it up, wound the stem and the second hand began to move. I put the watch in my pocket and a week later, when Gene Cox returned from his trip south, we were sitting at his kitchen table when I told him I had found something interesting on one of my walks.

"And what might that be?" he asked laconically.

I placed the watch on the table and Gene fell silent. He could not talk as he sat there looking at the watch in disbelief. After a long pause, he told me that it was his grandfather's watch. It had been given to his father, then to Gene, and a year earlier he had passed this family heirloom to his oldest son as a birthday present. Gene asked me where I found the watch. I described the area and he nodded his head. Three months earlier he had been horseback riding in the same area with his son. It was not until they returned to the homestead that his son realized he had lost the watch. They spent days looking for it before giving up the search. Gene reached for the watch and clenched it in his rough hands for a few moments. Then he looked up and said, "You and I don't have a whole lot in common, but I'll tell you one thing—you have just made a friend for life. You ever need a favor, you know who to ask."

The next morning Gene took me back to the Grand Hotel in the boat. Not much had changed in my absence. I moved back into my room and caught up on the repair work over the next few days. Shortly after my return, there was a going-away party for a schoolteacher who had miraculously completed her two-year contract. The public bar was filled to capacity with well-wishers, and during the course of the evening I fell into a lengthy conversation with the teacher who told me harrowing stories of how she survived the Thursday Island experience as a single, attractive white woman. She was going to leave Thursday Island early the following morning and so at the end of the evening I said goodbye and told her how much I enjoyed our conversation. She gave me a warm hug and a kiss and it was clear that both of us loved Thursday Island and the local people in the same way.

I went upstairs to my room at around midnight while the party was coming to an end. I undressed, turned off the light and climbed beneath my mosquito net. Like everyone else in the hotel, I always left my door ajar in order to catch the cool night air. Just as I was drifting off to sleep, I heard my door open. Illuminated by a dim shaft of light coming from the verandah I recognized the schoolteacher. In a very drunken state, she was in the corner of my room, leaning against the wall and trying to step out of her pants. I watched her unbutton her blouse, drop it to the floor and then reach behind her back to unclasp her bra. She slid her thumbs into the top of her panties and slid them over her hips. In our conversation at the bar, I figured I must have said something fairly brilliant to attract this sort of interest. My pulse raced but I couldn't imagine why she had selected me. Maybe it was because I was a stranger whom she would never see again. It was a mystery. But, instead of saying anything, I decided to simply lie back in bed and let her come to me.

No more than a minute passed before I felt the mosquito net part as someone sat down at the edge of my mattress. I opened my eyes, expecting to see the schoolteacher, but the schoolteacher was nowhere to be seen. Instead, the sobering vision of Goggle-eyed Tammy came into sharp focus. I caught my breath as she crawled toward me with that love light in her eyes—well, to be more accurate, with that love light in her one good eye. We wrestled for what seemed like several minutes before I got her off the bed and pinned her to the floor. I dragged Tammy out the door and down the verandah. I dumped her in front of the open door of a different man's room and then shoved her in.

Back in my room I locked my door and fell asleep wondering what had happened to the schoolteacher. By the time I went down for breakfast the next morning at 7:30, the schoolteacher was long gone, but everyone at the table already knew the story of what had happened the previous night. As it turned out, the teacher entered my room, thinking it was her own. Not until she was completely naked and standing next to the bed did she see me and realize that she was in the wrong room. She gathered her clothes in her arms and as she left my room, Tammy, who was on one of her nightly love patrols, caught sight of the naked woman. Tammy simply reasoned that she was next in line for whatever pleasures my room had to offer. There were no hard feelings between us because of my rough treatment. She was happy and content because she found what she was looking for in the other man's room.

Then one day, I suddenly left Thursday Island when I hitched a ride down the Great Barrier Reef on a visiting prawn trawler. I wanted to talk to friends in Sydney who had survived the cyclone, but I was worried about something else. Thursday Island was beginning to feel like home and I knew that if I stayed much longer, I might not leave. But there were other issues at work that led to my abrupt departure. For one, I couldn't imagine my time on the island getting any better, and so I convinced myself that it would be a good idea to leave before the bottom fell out of the experience. It was as if I was afraid the circus would leave town or that the magic would dry up and disappear. For most of my life I have felt like a human magnet for the sorts of people and experiences that I encountered at the Grand Hotel and on the islands of the Torres Strait. For years, I was convinced that it was perpetual motion that opened me up and made me vulnerable and receptive to odd and unusual encounters. For years, this compulsion to keep moving kept me on the road.

After an absence of twenty years, I'm not quite certain why I decided to go back to Thursday Island. Many experiences from this part of my life are far better left forgotten. But for unknowable reasons the people I met and the things that happened to me on Thursday Island and the islands of the Torres Strait were different. Long after I left the place, it continued to call to me. The call was so persistent that when a woman from the Australian Tourist Commission in Los Angeles called me in San Francisco to offer a magazine assignment to write about any place in the country, I knew immediately where I wanted to go: Thursday Island and the Grand Hotel. The idea was to promote tourism, but as I flew west across the Pacific Ocean I was lost in thought about Cyclone Tracy, the raw wild beauty of the Arnhem Land coast, and one of many nights I slept below deck on Big Black Ralph's pearling lugger the *Ruby Scarlet*. The first morning that I woke up on the

Ruby Scarlet I realized why the crew had slept on deck. My fingernails and toenails had been chewed to the quick by cockroaches. The traditional way to rid the luggers of these insects was to sink the boats in the mangroves for a few days each year and then refloat them after the cockroaches had abandoned ship. Obviously, the *Ruby Scarlet* was long overdue for its annual cockroach eradication treatment.

When I arrived back on Thursday Island in 1992, I wasn't sure what to expect. I was prepared for change, and the first thing I noticed was that the Grand Hotel had a public telephone with the handset and cord still attached. All of the rooms came with doors. A fax machine and a computer sat on the desk of a neat-looking office and it was possible to book a room in advance and pay with a credit card. A software program called Micromate Hospitality Systems organized everyday tasks such as "Saloon Accounting" and "Guest Management." In former times guest management had been limited to throwing drunks headfirst down the front steps.

The main structure of the Grand Hotel was built in 1890, in classic Queensland colonial style. A verandah ran around the top floor and the hip roof was covered with corrugated metal. Most of the wood-paneled rooms with their French doors, tall ceilings and overhead fans had now been restored to their original grandeur. Somerset Maugham had been a guest in May 1921, and lifelong Thursday Island resident Florie Kennedy remembered Douglas Fairbanks dining at the hotel with his wife, Lady Ashley, during a stopover on their yacht.

The hotel guest book testified to decades of spirited hospitality:

"Atmospheric."

"A harrowing good time was had by all."

"Never a dull moment."

"Good lord!"

"Over the top!"

"A great place to forget the rest of the world."

One hundred miles to the north, across the Torres Strait, lay the fetid mangrove coast of Papua New Guinea. My first night back at the Grand Hotel I tuned in to Radio Port Moresby to catch up on the latest "payback" negotiations between tribal groups. These settlements for murders or "accidental" deaths were calculated in terms of pigs, cassowary feathers, chickens, tobacco, money and tape players. A pregnant woman had been killed in a car crash, and the payback negotiations revolved around speculation as to whether the unborn child would have been a boy or a girl. The grieving family insisted on the higher compensation for the loss of a boy, while the family of the driver at fault argued that the child might have been a girl.

From my vantage point on the verandah of the Grand Hotel, the first morning of my return, I could almost see the northern tip of the Cape York Peninsula, thirty miles to the southeast. To the east, the Tuesday Islets were hidden from sight, but I could easily make out the low profile of Wednesday Island. To the west lay Friday Island, the former site of a leper colony and quarantine station, from 1887 to 1907.

Captain Cook sailed the HMS *Endeavour* through these waters in 1770, and a popular belief today is that as he sailed from east to west, he named Tuesday, Wednesday, Thursday, and Friday Island in the order of the days he landed on them. It was actually Captain Bligh who named Wednesday Island as he made his way to Timor in a twenty-three-foot-long open boat after the mutiny on the *Bounty* in 1789. Not until the hydrographic survey of 1848–49 did Owen Stanley, on the HMS *Rattlesnake*, name the adjoining islands Tuesday, Thursday, and Friday. In fact, the names of Thursday and Friday islands were reversed in the original survey. It wasn't until just before the charts were printed that someone at the British Admiralty decided to change the names around so that the days read neatly from east to west.

When I first saw the harbor of Thursday Island in 1975 it was filled with a fleet of the gaff-rigged ketches like Ralph Nona's *Ruby Scarlet*, known as pearling luggers. Those old wooden sailing ships, many of them more than one hundred feet long, were all that remained of a much larger fleet that early in the twentieth century had attracted pearl-shell divers from around the world. Until World War II there was a worldwide market for pearl shell, used for the manufacture of buttons. But with the development of plastics the demand for mother-of-pearl disappeared, and the industry that had sustained Thursday Island since the 1870s dwindled. A few sepia-tone photos from the pearling days were hung on the walls of the dining room at the Grand Hotel, but the most enduring symbols from that time are the crumbling gravestones of nearly a thousand divers in the cemetery on Thursday Island.

Today the major exports of the Torres Strait are frozen prawns and lobster tails. A few of the luggers are still in use, but the harbor is now dominated by an assortment of barges, steel-hulled fishing trawlers, yachts, aluminum dinghies (known as tinnies), the occasional coastal freighter, and the much less frequent cruise ship. The old brass helmets, lead-weighted boots, and canvas diving suits that used to lie on the decks of the luggers have long since been discarded or sold to visitors who come to see Thursday Island.

Douglas Street, the main business thoroughfare, is still graced by mango trees and, in the cool of the morning, people go about their errands along the shaded sidewalks. Local businessmen, barefoot and in shorts, carry briefcases that probably contain fishing line and fresh bait. Older men and women sit on wooden benches under the trees and pass the time visiting. The older women have a pleasant habit of greeting each other by kissing the back of their friend's hand and then pressing it to their own cheek.

Looking at the people on Thursday Island, it is difficult to guess their ethnic background. The original Torres Strait Islanders were Melanesian, but the pearl-shell industry created a boomtown situation that attracted workers from the ends of the earth. Okinawans, Micronesians, Chinese, Malays, Indonesians, Sinhalese, Indians, Polynesians, mainland Aborigines, tribesmen from Papua New Guinea, Europeans, Torres Strait Islanders, Filipinos, Russians, and assorted vagabonds from points unknown intermingled to produce a community where a Japanese Muslim or a Pentecostalist of Latvian-Aboriginal ancestry is not considered unusual.

The main downtown area looked much cleaner than I recalled, despite the discarded liquor bottles. Broken and empty liquor bottles have been a feature of the landscape since Thursday Island was first settled by Europeans in the mid-nineteenth century. Glass shards still litter the surface of the beaches on Thursday Island and reach a depth of several feet. By 1885 one of the island's most notable sights was the gigantic mound of bottles that had formed behind Thomas McNulty's bar. The cone-shaped mass of liquor bottles was said to be taller than the coconut palms or any building on the island at the time. Observing the pile during an unofficial visit to McNulty's bar, Government Resident (and later Queensland Premier) John Douglas commented that the mound "testified to the achievements of those who had lived on the island in prehistoric times."

On my first Sunday morning back on Thursday Island I was looking for ripe mangoes in the trees along Douglas Street when I heard a distant booming. I followed the sound and eventually took a seat in the rear pew of the Anglican church. The large congregation was belting out island hymns to the accompaniment of a big bass drum and tambourines made of beer-bottle caps strung on wire coat hangers. Eventually the entire congregation, along with the band, stood up and circled the inside of the church clapping and singing.

At the conclusion of the service, I decided to look up my old friend Alfie Mills. I had met him in the Grand Hotel in 1975, but I didn't know where he lived. I left a message for him with the bartender and the next morning Alfie called by the hotel to invite me home for lunch with his wife, Ella. Dozens of large plastic fishing floats hung like Christmas ornaments from the trees in their front yard. The walls of their living room were lined with the photos and mementos of a lifetime: Alfie's days as a pearl diver, Ella as a beautiful young woman, old friends, portraits of their adopted children, and black-and-white snapshots of family picnics and celebrations.

Alfie, whose grandfather came from Samoa, is one of the most respected old divers on Thursday Island. Ella's father came from the island of Sulawesi. For lunch she served us an Indonesian-style meal of coconut-milk curries, steamed rice, spicy sambals, krupuk (deep-fried prawn crackers), as well as island specialties such as barbecued dugong and sautéed pearl-shell meat. Dried pearl-shell meat is one of the most coveted ingredients for Chinese soups and other dishes. The flavor is similar, but far superior, to that of a scallop. In specialty stores on the Australian mainland it sells for around $500 a kilo, but on Thursday Island this delicacy is a common gift.

As we ate, Alfie reminisced about his work on the pearling luggers. He started diving when he was twelve and he survived thirty-four years on the boats. Seven of those years were spent working the most treacherous areas, like the Darnley Deeps out near the Great Barrier Reef.

From my first visit to Thursday Island I remembered stories told by other old divers who hung around the Grand Hotel. I had heard how, as young men, they went out to sea for months at a time, living on a diet of tinned pickled beef, salted fish, rice, and fresh pearl-shell meat. These men would climb into heavy canvas diving suits with bronze helmets and lead-weighted shoes and pray that the air compressors wouldn't stop when they were at thirty to fifty fathoms searching for giant silver-lip and gold-lip pearl shell. Venomous sea snakes, sharks, giant groupers, eighteen-foot-long saltwater crocodiles, and burst eardrums didn't worry the divers nearly as much as the possibility that their air hoses would get tangled or cut by the ship's propeller.

In 1957 Alfie was gathering pearl shell at forty fathoms when he heard the air compressor on his ship slow down. He wasn't getting enough oxygen, and he soon broke out in a cold sweat.

"My right side began to go numb," he said. "Split me right down the middle. I was paralyzed on the right side. Half of my brain must have gone too. My right eye didn't work.

"I yanked on my rope once, the signal for my tender to pull me up, and then I passed out. By the time they got me on deck I was in bad shape. I had the bends. I was sick and frightened, I ached all over, but the skipper, he knew what to do. He saved my life.

"He put the helmet back on me and sent me down to slowly decompress in stages. I didn't want to go. It was sunset, and they lowered me down to thirty fathoms again. I stayed there for three hours, then they pulled me up to five fathoms for another four hours. I was cold and hungry. I got sick in my helmet and diving suit. In the dark the sharks came, and when they turned quickly, the phosphorescence illuminated the inside of my helmet. I just hung there all night watching those lights in front of my face.

"When they pulled me up, I was all right. I could see out of my right eye, and the next day I started diving again.

"But that was nothing," Alfie continued. "We all had our troubles. During the 1937 season, Iona Asai, a diver from Saibai Island, was attacked by a shark. It took his head and one shoulder in its mouth and didn't let go until Iona stuck his thumbs in the shark's eyes. It took more than two hundred stitches to patch up the holes in his neck and shoulder, but Iona lived. He's still around."

Before I left their home that afternoon, I asked Alfie what had happened to the three big island mammas who used to play ukuleles and sing at the Federal Hotel. "You must be talkin' about my sisters," he laughed. "They're still performing. They been at it for thirty years now."

Every Wednesday night on Thursday Island, the Mills Sisters sing old island songs and popular ballads at the nearby Federal Hotel, which faces the waterfront on Victoria Parade. The night I went to listen to them I didn't see anyone performing backflips from the pool table or blowing fireballs with mouthfuls of kerosene, but by ten P.M. the crowd included the familiar mix of island residents enjoying a typical night on the town.

Grizzled fishermen opened beer bottles with their teeth, while middle-aged government officials with hairpieces and white knee socks sipped rum and Cokes and talked about "blackfellas." Tattooed dockworkers and crayfish divers flirted with the young women. Distinguished-looking older couples sat quietly at tables and enjoyed the singing and a few dances before heading home hand in hand, along dark, dusty streets that still gave off the heat from late afternoon.

The Mills Sisters were dressed in voluminous flower-print dresses. They sang for hours and provided a soothing counterpoint to the intense intermingling of friends and strangers. The most riveting exchange came from a man who was arguing with himself. Over the course of fifteen minutes he became increasingly agitated and incoherent until he suddenly stormed outside and started butting his head against the hood of a parked car. I'm uncertain who won the argument, but, having made his point, the man returned to his table where he serenaded a stuffed doll with his harmonica. He spent the rest of the evening nursing a beer and mumbling to the doll. No one reacted to the man, and I somehow found it reassuring to know that this sort of behavior was still an accepted way of life on the island.

Just after sunrise a few mornings later, Alfie brought his son's dinghy to the public wharf. We loaded tins of fuel, hand spools of fishing lines, and an ice chest full of sandwiches, fruit, water and fresh bait. I untied the bowline and we headed south down the channel between Horn and Prince of Wales Islands. Buffeted by the southeast trade winds, we made slow progress for the first hour until we rounded the southern end of Prince of Wales. There, protected from the wind and ocean swell, we anchored in the lee of a small island. Alfie fished, while I went ashore to collect oysters exposed by the low tide. We ate the oysters raw, shared a cold beer and then continued on to Packe Island. A Chinese junk was washed up on the beach, but three barking German shepherd dogs prevented us from venturing ashore to investigate.

We followed the southwest coast of Prince of Wales Island and stopped to fish along the way. In 1975 people still hunted for wild pig and deer on the island but today Prince of Wales is mainly a public recreational reserve. You can no longer hunt, but local fish such as coral trout, mackerel, mullet, and barramundi are easy to catch on hand lines. Watching the green coastline slip by, I was suddenly reminded of the needs of the Australian Tourist Commission. It occurred to me that with a sea kayak, a tent and basic supplies, one could spend weeks poking around the islands, playing at being Robinson Crusoe. But then again, there was probably adventure enough simply sitting at the bar of the Grand Hotel, talking to the likes of Goggle-eyed Tammy and playing at being Charles Bukowski.

As I daydreamed, Alfie pointed out the graceful tamarind trees and coconut palms that originally had been planted by seasonal bêche-de-mer fishermen from Indonesia. From offshore we could also see the white flowers of the wongai tree. The trees grow wild on most islands and from my time on Prince of Wales I remembered the sweet dark-brown fruit that tasted much like a plum but with the smooth texture of a fresh date.

By early afternoon we had tied up at a small wooden dock on the east side of Friday Island. Alfie sat in the dinghy and continued to fill the ice chest with fish, as I went in search of Kazuyoshi Takami, co-owner of a cultured pearl farm on the island. Apart from a camp of squatters on the north coast, he and his Japanese partner had the island to themselves. Kazuyoshi was brought up in Japan, but at the time of my visit he had lived on Friday Island for eighteen years. Once a month he flew down to Cairns to visit his wife and two children. The rest of the time he worked on the oyster farm—implanting nuclei inside the shells, then tending the 10,000 oysters placed in wire baskets and suspended from oil-drum rafts for the two or three years it takes to make a cultured pearl.

In 1971 an oil spill ravaged the oyster rafts, and diseases continue to decimate the oyster population. To replenish his stock Kazuyoshi buys live pearl shell locally, at about $14 each, but it is only a matter of time before the last pearl-shell farms go out of business. We ate a lunch of cold Japanese soba noodles with shredded nori and sesame seed oil, grilled fish, and pearl-shell meat. Then Kazuyoshi and I sat on the front porch and looked at the oyster rafts anchored in a long line. We talked about island life.

"Where else can you enjoy such solitude?" Kazuyoshi asked.

"Solitude" was not the word that immediately leapt to mind when I thought about my range of experiences in the Torres Strait Islands, but I nodded my head in agreement.

On the far side of the channel, I could just make out the entrance to Northwest Creek. Twenty years earlier I had used that winding waterway through the mangroves to reach the one-room homestead where I worked for Gene Cox. Sitting with Kazuyoshi, I remembered the night I pulled a wet tarp over my back and saved the tractor by driving it through a wall of fire to safe ground that had already been burned. On a hot afternoon, halfway up the creek, I was standing up in the boat, looking out for submerged branches, when a mullet jumped into the air and hit me square in the chest. The fish fell to the floor of the boat and that night I had fried mullet for dinner. On other nights I sat beneath a canopy of stars and listened to the BBC *World News Report*. I could still remember the smell of the flowering wattle trees, and the simple pleasure of being awakened at first light by the far-off laughter of a kookaburra. That had all happened such a long time ago, but I found myself suddenly caught up in a flood of memories.

I thought about Alfie and Kazuyoshi and the denizens of the Grand Hotel. How profoundly different my life would have been if I had decided to stay on the islands. I could have easily found work on the fishing boats or as a carpenter or builder on Thursday Island. My mind was filled with twenty years' worth of imaginary opportunities lost and gained. I walked with Kazuyoshi to the wharf, where Alfie was sitting in the sun laughing. He gently yanked his fishing line and smiled to himself. Kazuyoshi handed Alfie a bag of dried pearl-shell meat. We cast off our mooring lines and at sunset we crossed the main shipping channel and returned to Thursday Island for one last evening at the Grand Hotel.

Some people say you can never go home or return to a place once loved, or recapture a friendship left behind. Time, life, circumstances and fate all have their way of changing who we are and altering beyond all recognition memories or feelings until they finally seem like part of a dream or an illusion. But I knew I had to go back to Thursday Island and I am glad that I didn't wait any longer than I did. A few months after my visit I received a short note from Alfie Mills. He had news for me. An early-morning fire had swept through the wood-frame structure of the Grand Hotel and burned it to the ground.

LISTENING TO THE KAVA

IT WAS A QUIET MORNING on the coast. Listening to the sound of distant surf pounding on the black sand beach I realized I was awake. A warm sea breeze blew through the walls of the bamboo bungalow and when I opened my eyes I looked up at the thatched roof and remembered I was on Tanna, one of the outer islands of Vanuatu. A truck approached on the gravel road. Stones spat from beneath the tires and the vehicle skidded to a stop.

The previous night I had stayed up late, talking with Chief Tom Numake. He told me a long story of how his great-grandfather used magic stones to call the big sea turtles onto the beach at night where they were captured alive by a line of bare-breasted women dressed in grass skirts. The turtles were rubbed with coconut cream and then carried by men to the inland villages as peace offerings. Sacred turtle trails once radiated from a nearby banyan tree to link the coastal villages with those of the highlands. The magic turtle stones were passed on to Chief Tom, but he did not know the proper incantations and, in any event, the people no longer had any use for turtle offerings. Tribal raids were a thing of the past. During my visit in 1985, the islanders drove around the island in dilapidated cars, ate tinned food and went to church. Chief Tom knew the old stories, but he spent most of his time going over the accounts of his small goods shop that served the local fishing villages. I tried to envision the scene of naked men carrying live giant turtles through the forest in the moonlight, but what I remembered most from my talk with Chief Tom was his story about a drink called kava.

In the beginning, according to Chief Tom, there was no night, only day. Then Kalpawapen, a jungle deity, came down from atop Mount Tukosmere and gave the Tannese men a cicada, a rooster and kava. The cicada's chirping sent the sun below the horizon and the next morning the rooster's crow announced the first sunrise. Kava drinking gave men a direct link with the spirit world and access to mystical power.

The daily kava ceremony is the major social event for men on Tanna. On this remote island the cultivation and consumption of kava (*Piper methysticum*) is surrounded by mystery. Magic stones, found in the black volcanic soil, are used to ensure a good crop. Women are prohibited from drinking kava and they are not allowed to watch as the men partake. The punishment used to be death if a woman observed the kava ceremony, but today a fine of one pig is considered sufficient. These prohibitions seemed odd to me, since island legends told how the first kava root was found growing in a woman's vagina. It was unclear if this was where Kalpawapen had made his discovery, and Chief Tom was vague on this point. There were other restrictions regarding the kava ceremony. Only circumcised virgin boys were allowed to squeeze the liquid from the masticated kava root; and strictly speaking, only married men should drink kava. As I understood it, each evening the men gathered at the village *nakamal*, the dance ground, to prepare and drink kava. Then all those present would fall silent as they "listened to the kava."

Before going to bed that night I asked Chief Tom if I could visit the kava gardens in a remote village. He said he would take care of everything. As I slept he sent one of his sons to make arrangements for the following morning.

A horn sounded. It was seven A.M.

Climbing from beneath my mosquito net I fastened a sarong around my waist and looked out the door. An elderly black man waved from the cab of a battered truck. I waved back and the man lifted his hand in greeting and nodded. My transportation had arrived. I splashed water in my face and dressed quickly. Slamming the truck door closed behind me, I slid onto the front seat and shook hands with Moses, my driver. He touched two bare wires together, the engine grumbled to life, and for the next hour the vehicle rattled along a rough dirt track that wound its way into the mountains.

Nestled in the central mountains of Tanna, surrounded by tropical rain forest, was Middle Bush, the jungle village of Chief Samson Kasso. This was our destination. Middle Bush is distinguished from the other villages on the island by the extraordinary amount of garden space set aside for the cultivation of kava. The varieties of kava grown on Tanna are generally regarded as the most potent in the South Pacific, and Middle Bush enjoys a well-earned reputation for having the best kava on the island.

As I climbed down from the truck Moses promised to pick me up at sunset. The truck drove off and I was left standing at the side of the road wondering what to do next. There wasn't a building or person in sight. Before long, a young man playing a bamboo panpipe appeared from the forest. He wore nothing but a pandanus-fiber penis wrapper that looked like an inverted whisk broom or miniature grass skirt concealing an engorged member. This cluster of straw-colored fibers is called a *nambas*. For many of the older village men, the nambas makes up their entire wardrobe. I handed the boy my letter of introduction from Chief Tom and as he read the letter I occupied myself by looking at the chicken feathers carefully arranged upright in his kinky brown hair.

"Welcome to Middle Bush, sir," he said.

"Thank you," I replied, trying to conceal my astonishment at his excellent English.

I followed my young guide into the forest. Mynah birds twittered in the branches overhead as we stepped over the buttressed tree roots. The forest floor was carpeted with a russet-colored leaf fall and the smoke of cooking fires hung in the cool morning air. Weak shafts of sunlight filtered through the canopy of trees and I could see the dappled figures of people moving through the undergrowth. With digging sticks carried over their shoulders, they padded silently down slick, foot-worn jungle pathways to the garden plots. We walked for a short while before arriving at the hut of Yallu Kasso, the chief's son. The hut, set at the edge of a clearing, was a rough affair of thick posts supporting a roof of thatch. The walls were left open for ventilation and chickens pecked about the immaculate cooking area. Yallu Kasso spoke English and Pidgin as well as the island dialect. He was dressed in a khaki field shirt tucked into a flowered sarong tied at his waist.

Yallu Kasso apologized that his father would be gone for the day, but he told me that he would be honored to take me on a tour of the kava gardens. The village received few visitors and soon after my arrival a large group of chattering men and boys, all dressed in nambas, had assembled at Yallu Kasso's hut. Before leaving for the kava gardens, Yallu Kasso suggested I take off my shoes. When I asked him why he told me that without shoes I could feel the warmth of the earth. This seemed like a reasonable request and so I put my shoes in my shoulder bag and soon we were walking barefoot, single file, down one of the narrow footpaths.

Our first stop was at the chief's yam hut. Peering into the dimly lit interior I saw what looked like an assortment of logs arranged in a row on the dirt floor. The logs turned out to be giant yams. Two of the men selected a six-foot-long monster and held it up for my approval. It must have weighed at least fifty pounds.

"Nice one," I said.

Who knows what sort of recipe would call for one of these yams. Peel? Grate? Mash? Slice and deep-fry? Julienne? Or maybe just wrap the thing in a blanket of banana leaves and heave it into a pit with white-hot stones and a whole pig. Anything less than a village feast would create weeks, maybe months' worth of leftover giant yam.

The chief's kava garden was next. Crouched on the ground in the cool air beneath the green canopy of the kava leaves, Yallu Kasso explained that kava takes approximately five years to grow to maturity. Multiple stalks, two inches in diameter, reach a height of about seven feet, and are crowned with a dense growth of green leaves. Bent over double, we moved further into the garden as the men pointed out the different types of kava. The climate and soil conditions in Middle Bush are ideal; three of the fourteen types of kava grown there are so strong that after a few sips it is impossible to walk. One type is so powerful that it is no longer taken because of the wild hallucinations that it can produce.

As for the kava types still in common use, there was kava Far-ay, Ne Kow-Apin, Wa Pa-Hill, Neka-oapia, Kamitah, Ne Kis-Kis Nean, Mala-Mala, Bama, Sow-Sow, Do-Dey, Tuan and Wok-Let. *Wok-Let* is Pidgin for "work late" and it is said that if you drink kava Wok-Let you will arrive at work late the following day.

A special chief's kava known as Sumarian is cultivated by raising the young plant above the ground in such a way that the sucker roots at the base cannot develop. This technique of air-pruning produces a central taproot that is three to four feet long and seven inches wide. Kava Tapunga is another type of kava reserved for the chiefs. No one else is allowed to touch the plant. The example I was shown had been planted in a hollowed section of palm trunk set into the ground. This was another way of developing the large, desirable central root that is the most potent section of the plant. Kava roots are sold in the open-air village markets as a cash crop, but kava is also used as ceremonial gifts and for sharing with friends. Eighty vatu (80 cents U.S.) will buy a kilo of average quality kava. Three kilos of this sort of kava is enough for five men.

As we walked through dense forest on our way to a more

distant kava plot we came upon a timid-looking man standing at the edge of the trail. He appeared undecided whether to stay or run. He had light-brown skin, straight black hair and oriental features that were markedly different from my stocky, dark-skinned Melanesian companions.

"Who is that?" I asked.

"That man?" Yallu Kasso said. "That man crazy. He come from Java."

"Java, Indonesia?"

"Hmmm . . . might be," he replied uncertainly.

"*Pandai bahasa Indonesia?* [Do you speak Indonesian?]" I asked the man, who was cowering in the bushes.

Partially concealed by the undergrowth, the man stood there as if he was ready to run. A look of confused disbelief wrinkled his face. It took him a moment to digest what I had said, and to reply to my question. "*Pandai* [I speak it]," the man finally stammered, seemingly shocked by the sound of his own words. His name was Ngaderoan Neheru, but everyone knew him as Bob.

The others fell silent as I talked to Bob. He had not spoken his own language in twenty-five years and the other men were mystified that I could communicate with him. I learned that Bob had been born in 1915 near Pangandaran, a small fishing village on the south coast of central Java. In the years following World War II he worked on merchant ships that carried him around the world six times. In 1950 he spent one week in New York City, and two days in San Francisco. He eventually drifted to Tanna where he married a local woman. She bore him five children before leaving him for another man in the village. This was acceptable to Bob, who said he preferred living by himself. According to his own estimate he had fathered an additional twenty children in various other countries.

When Bob first arrived in Middle Bush, his wife's home village, he tried adapting to the local custom of drinking kava every afternoon. He found the drink too strong, but he persevered because on Tanna a man who does not attend the daily kava drinking ceremony excludes himself from the most important social event shared by the men. While the kava roots are being prepared the men conduct the equivalent of a casual mini town meeting. After a year Bob gave up kava drinking. He realized this would make him less of a man and a fringe dweller in his adopted community, but he preferred being a social outcast to the debilitating aftereffects of drinking Tannese kava every day. Bob didn't own land and he did not work in the gardens. This set him apart even further from the other men. But he managed to make himself useful by repairing wind-up alarm clocks, radios and old shotguns. His presence was tolerated, but he was largely ignored.

Bob was seventy years old when I met him. He lived in a hut by himself with no nearby neighbors. His children had moved to the coast or to the capital, Vila, on the most important island, Éfaté, to find work. The villagers of Middle Bush were generous and they had fed and taken care of Bob for the previous fifteen years. As he had withdrawn into memories of a world unknown to people around him, the villagers assumed Bob had grown mute or feebleminded. In recent years he had spoken infrequently, but when faced with the opportunity to speak his own language with me he became animated and excited.

"Tell the men about the big buildings, the concrete and the cars," Bob pleaded. I didn't immediately understand the significance of his request until he explained that he had been ridiculed for years because of stories he had told of a world beyond the island. The villagers had long since laughed off his accounts of daily life in Manhattan as the fabrications of a madman or a liar. This was not surprising. Few of the people from Middle Bush had traveled as far as the other side of the island. Until recently, a trip to Yasur Volcano, a distance of about ten miles in a straight line, was considered to be the journey of a lifetime.

I told Yallu Kasso and the others that there were buildings in America twice as tall as Yasur Volcano. Long metal trucks with a hundred wheels ran through tunnels in the earth carrying thousands of people. It was a city of glass and concrete and steel where holes had to be cut into the stone footpaths so that trees could grow. I described a land where ice fell from the sky and where it was illegal to keep chickens and pigs in the house. There was no soil set aside for gardening, no kava, and there were no giant yams. I measured a short distance between my two index fingers to indicate the modest size of yams in America. Yallu Kasso and the others shook their heads and made guttural clucking sounds as they contemplated these hard facts.

"You call that a yam?" one man scoffed.

"No kava gardens? Illegal chickens?" a second man asked, to make sure he had understood me correctly.

Bob smiled, satisfied that after twenty-five years the truth was known. He wanted me to stay and talk but my guides were eager to show me the taro and tapioca fields, and it would soon be time to dig up and prepare the kava. I stayed with Bob long enough to describe modern Jakarta, which he had not seen since 1946. But then it was time to go. Bob asked me to come back and talk to him again soon. He wasn't crazy at all, just old and lonely.

Before sunset, Yallu Kasso and I walked to the nakamal, where a dozen older men had already gathered to cut and clean the kava roots. I met Chief Samson Kasso, a dignified-looking older man dressed in double-pleated blue cotton drill shorts and a plaid dress shirt unbuttoned to the waist. Young boys were busy gnawing the kava roots to a soft, fibrous mush before disgorging mouthfuls of the stuff onto saucer-sized leaves. It was not an appetizing sight. Each sodden gray pile, consisting of three mouthfuls, equaled one serving—and one of those servings had my name on it.

The cocktail hour finally arrived. One of the boys mixed a pile of the masticated kava with water, then twisted it in a mat of coconut fibers. The resulting brown beverage filtered through the fibers and dripped into a coconut-shell cup. Chief Samson Kasso did the honors. He drained the first cup in one quick motion then, turning his back to the rest of us, he strode purposefully to the edge of the dance ground and blew a small spray of liquid into the bushes. He uttered an invocation to the agricultural deity Mwatiktik for good luck and good crops. The chief made a loud, clear cry into the jungle to complete the ritual. He touched the cup to the ground to ensure the strength of the kava stayed with the drinker. The cup was refilled and then handed to me.

I looked into the cup and caught my breath. "Bottoms up," I thought to myself. I started drinking and the taste was shocking—like a blend of viscous muddy water, another person's saliva and composted lawn trimmings. Wine-tasting terminology came to mind. Astringent and chewy . . . with vibrant notes of pulverized tree bark or privet hedge put through a wood chipper. Herbaceous and musty with a distinctly earthy finish. I thought I might retch, but at the third or fourth gulp my mouth and tongue went numb, followed by my throat and stomach. I felt the strength go out of my knees. I walked to the edge of the clearing, spit out a feeble spray of kava onto my shirt front, mumbled a few reverent-sounding noises in imitation of Chief Samson Kasso and let out the best Tarzan yell I could manage. By the time I touched the cup to the ground I was already feeling funny. The other men drank, yelled into the jungle, and then within a very short while the conversation faded until the last whispered comments and the sounds of the chirping cicadas blended into one solid buzzing tone in my head.

Flowering bushes and aromatic shrubs sent a fragrance across the now hushed dance ground. My eyes had difficulty shifting from near to far focus and my body pounded with each heartbeat. I felt myself drifting deeper and deeper into a secret world of gardens and dreams, male rituals . . . and the unknown. I felt an overwhelming affinity for my fellow drinkers, but in the gathering darkness the men wandered off separately to the far edges of the jungle clearing to abandon themselves to their kava dreams. The sensation of sitting perfectly still in the jungle twilight was utterly euphoric. "Drinking kava," Yallu Kasso had told me earlier, "is like shaking hands in farewell." This was true. We never spoke again.

At the first sound of the truck, I lost my sense of timelessness and fell into a panic. I wasn't ready to leave, but in typical Western fashion, I didn't want to deviate from the original plan by making my driver wait. I forgot that we were on Melanesian Standard Time. As Moses quietly approached, I staggered to my feet and mumbled, "We can go now." He took one look at me and said, "You should sit down and listen to the kava."

I wasn't sure exactly what the kava was saying to the other men, but I had a pretty good idea based on my adrenaline rush and growing sense of excitement and blind fear as I felt myself hurtling to the edge of an abyss beyond which I knew I would either fly or plummet head over heels through time and space.

The jungle began to spin and the next moment I dropped to the ground as if felled by a wooden pig club. I lay on the cool, packed earth for the next thirty minutes unable to speak. During that time it became abundantly clear why kava had been used as a peace offering. Who could lift a weapon in such a state? I also realized why missionary opposition to kava drinking had been so strong: it was pure drug-induced bliss. Kava drinking with these men seemed like the ultimate communion with self and nature and the cosmos. Male bonding in its purest form. My imagination careened out of control. I began to hallucinate and I wondered if I would ever come back to the person I thought I once was. Sometime later, assisted by three phantom shapes, I managed to walk to the truck in the darkness. Moses drove into the night and it didn't take me long to figure out that driving on winding mountain roads and kava drinking do not mix. Halfway back to the coast I had Moses stop the truck so that I could make an unscheduled second invocation to Mwatiktik. I lurched to the edge of the road, fell to my hands and knees and vomited into a ditch. When I climbed back into the truck I thought I would start feeling better, but to my horror I realized the kava was just starting to kick in.

Standing in front of my bungalow, I fumbled for my room key and then, from a prudent ten feet away, I lined up the key with the door lock. Moses provided me with an opportunity to regain some dignity by letting me cover this last stretch unassisted. With the key held firmly in my right hand, I carefully walked into the side of the bamboo hut more than three feet to the right of the keyhole. I vaguely remember the sound of Moses laughing as the truck drove off.

Four hours later the kava was still speaking. Geckos chirped loudly on the ceiling of the bungalow as I lay flat on my back laughing—covered in perspiration. Adrift in a sea of wild visions, I saw myself barefoot wandering the sacred turtle trails with a procession of Tannese warriors. Like the other men, my buttocks were bared and my dick was wrapped up in a nambas. The warm stiffened straw felt good against my skin. Glistening female bodies were dancing all around me, nudging me with their shoulders, their hips, their breasts and thighs. There was the swishing sound of grass skirts, laughter and the intoxicating sweet sensual scent of women aroused. Everywhere I looked there were clapping hands, swaying hips and jiggling firm brown breasts with stiffened nipples. Overwhelmed by the jostling of hot, wet, undulating bodies all around me, I felt myself go hard and thanked God I was wearing the nambas.

Down on the beach, I thought I heard the sound of conch shells being blown, but I didn't have the strength or the will to get up to investigate. It was all I could do to keep pace with the hallucinations of what looked like twelve-foot-long geckos fornicating upside down on the ceiling and attacking mosquitoes the size of seagulls. Moments of darkness mingled with dreams of wandering across a forest clearing bathed in silvery moonlight. People were laughing or screaming. I couldn't tell if the sounds were coming from outside my hut or from inside my head, and at some point I fell unconscious.

A rooster's crow announced the unwelcome dawn and hours later Chief Tom found me slouched in a chair on the verandah gazing blankly into a cup of cold tea covered with floating gnats. I hadn't brushed my teeth or changed my clothes from the night before. I vaguely remember wondering how many other strangers had ever had such an experience, and if I ever wanted to have another one. With feigned innocence, Chief Tom asked me how the tour of the Middle Bush kava gardens had gone the previous afternoon. I thumbed through my crumpled and mud-stained notebook until I read out my last scribbled entry.

"Tonight we drank kava Do-Dey."

Chief Tom laughed with delight and replied, "Not Do-Dey, what you drank is called kava Two-Day. If you took that one you will not recover for two days."

Chief Tom spoke the truth.

Night Fishing with
Nahimah

THE SHORT RUNWAY took up the entire length and width
of the island and by the time the propeller-driven Air
India plane lurched to an abrupt stop we were perched at the
very edge of an endless indigo sea. The plane slowly turned
around, then taxied to an open-air hut that served as the
Republic of Maldives International Airport Terminal on Hul-
ule Island. The date was June 14th, 1977. I walked across the
tarmac beneath a midday sky filled with flat-bottomed, dense
white clouds and then entered the terminal. No one looked at
my passport and the customs formalities were limited to a
handwritten sign taped to the wall that read: "Condoms,
Alcohol and Images of the Buddha Are Prohibited in the
Republic of Maldives. Please Enjoy Your Stay." I picked up
my bag and during the short ferryboat ride to the main island
of Male (pronounced *Mal-ay*) I realized the rumors had been
true. I could stay for as long as I wanted. This fit my plans
well, because I had come to the Maldives to buy dried fish and
smuggle them to Sri Lanka.

In my pocket I had the address of my local contact, a man by the name of Don Tutu. I met Don Tutu later that afternoon as he stood in the doorway of his single story coralblock home. The house was barely two hundred yards from where he had been born years earlier. When he was younger, Don Tutu had been the sultan's drummer. His father and grandfather had also been drummers, but the sultanate of the Maldives had been abolished in 1968 and because of Don Tutu's aching knee joints and the lack of royal ceremonies he now drummed only once a year, on the president's birthday. He spent a good deal of his time smoking cigars and consulting on the export of the country's most valuable commodity—*Katsuwonus pelamis*, the skipjack tuna. Sun-dried and smoked, it is known as Maldive fish. The local name was *hikikandumas*.

Don Tutu called his family compound the Drummer's Shelter. The compound, made up of two bungalows and a detached kitchen, was surrounded by rough coral walls six feet high and completely shaded by coconut palms, mango, guava, lime and breadfruit trees. In order to bring in extra income the smaller bungalow was often rented out to Sri Lankan small-goods smugglers who dealt in dried Maldive fish, polyester saris, calculators, fountain pens, perfumed talcum powder, bolts of wash-and-wear trouser material, cassette players, Wilkinson Sword double-edged razor blades, family-sized tins of powdered milk and Nescafé instant coffee. These, and other import duty-free items, were taken to Colombo, the capital of Sri Lanka, by a small army of transient smugglers who lived as seasonal residents on Male. I intended to become a part of this group, partially for the money, but mainly because I knew, from years of travel throughout the Middle East and Asia, that the best way to penetrate a culture and mingle with the people was by getting involved with the local economy.

I didn't have any interest in trading cases of talcum powder or instant coffee because of the large volume of these commodities and the small profit margins. Maldive fish, however, was another matter. Customs duties for Maldive fish in Sri Lanka were high, but according to rumor there were many ways to get the fish around the official ports of entry in order to sell directly to restaurants or individuals. I had never seen or tasted Maldive fish before I arrived in Male, but Don Tutu confirmed what I had heard: the fish was in great demand because it was an essential ingredient in Sri Lankan cuisine. Maldive fish is cheap and abundant in Male. In Colombo, I had been told I could pretty well name my price if I brought the very best quality. I planned on purchasing burlap bags full of dried fish once I understood where to buy it and how to determine quality. After I explained my intentions, Don Tutu gave me the names of a few dealers in wholesale Maldive fish down near the wharf.

My second day on Male I visited the island library, where I discovered a 1940 first-edition folio of H.C.P. Bell's *The Maldive Islands: Monograph on the History, Archaeology, and Epigraphy*. The meticulously detailed descriptions provided me with a concise historical and cultural overview of the place where I planned to live for the coming months. In addition to advising me on Maldive fish, Don Tutu had a special interest in the folklore and social history of the Maldives, and he became my other major source of information. The Maldives are made up of approximately 1,200 coral islands, contained within a chain of twenty-six atolls that begin about 300 miles west of the tip of India and extend south, for nearly 480 miles, to just below the equator. Strategically located on the ancient trade-wind route between the Arabian Peninsula and Sri Lanka and Asia, the low coral islands and uncharted maze of submerged reefs have been a dangerous barrier to traditional sailing dhows as well as modern shipping. The main island, Male, at 1.7 square kilometers, is the largest island by far with a modern population of approximately 55,000 people. According to Bell, in 1153 a North African by the name of Abu al-Barakat killed a virgin-hungry monster by reciting verses from the Koran. Ever since then, the islanders have followed the teachings of Islam. I also learned that from around 500 BC until the arrival of Islam the islanders were Buddhists. Sorcery and magic were connected to an earlier animist religion known as *fandhita*—which, according to Don Tutu and others, was still practiced. Despite the jumble of fact and fiction, it was clear to me that the Maldives enjoyed an ancient, rich and varied culture, relatively free from European colonial influences.

I needed a place to stay while I learned about the fish trade and as luck would have it, a week after I arrived in Male, the small bungalow at the Drummer's Shelter became vacant. I paid two months' rent in advance and moved in. One of the Sri Lankan smugglers, who was dressed like a South Asian version of Elvis Presley during his Las Vegas period, stopped by the Drummer's Shelter one afternoon to talk to Don about a new scheme to move large quantities of Maldive fish to Colombo in small boats. Don Tutu dismissed the smuggler with a polite wave of his hand, and the man walked off muttering to himself while touching up his heavily pomaded hair with a long, thin comb.

"A big talker," said Don. "As we say in Male, 'He's all foreskin.'"

My first night on the island I had walked along the eastern waterfront at sunset. I found a local restaurant where I ordered the only dish being served—a plate of curried Maldive fish and rice. As I waited for my meal, I noticed that my place mat was a neatly torn half-page from the *San Francisco Chronicle,* my hometown newspaper. The page was six months old and on it I found a classified ad with the heading "Invitation to a Killing." For two dollars I could buy an original document "suitable for framing" for this "unique double execution" to be held at San Quentin's gas chamber. I reached across the table to inspect a different newspaper place mat. I read a story about the recent rezoning of salamanders in Santa Cruz County, California, statistics on random street shootings in San Francisco, and the details of a pre-Thanksgiving hijack of a truck carrying 12,000 frozen turkey carcasses valued at $32,000. I had been gone from San Francisco for nearly five years at this point, but judging from the news in front of me it didn't sound like I was missing out on very much.

My dinner was brought to the table and while I was coming to terms with my first bite I decided that the oily, dense red flesh with its concentrated fish flavor was an acquired taste. I felt as if I was eating something like very large, dried anchovies. Without the mound of steaming rice to help distribute the overpowering taste, I would have been hard-pressed to finish my dinner. I got up from the table and walked back to the Drummer's Shelter perplexed as to why there was such a huge demand for Maldive fish.

I later learned that the very highest grade of Maldive fish was ground to a powder and used in very small quantities, mainly to add complexity and depth of flavor and to bind other ingredients in a subtle but distinctive way. Maldive fish smells and tastes similar to *belachan*, the legendary fermented prawn paste of Malaysia and Indonesia. But perhaps a more closely related example is the Japanese condiment *katsuobushi magokoro*, the dried shaved bonito flakes commonly used in miso soup. For whatever reasons, the Sri Lankans were evidently addicted to Maldive fish and that is all I really needed to know.

Don Tutu took me to the fish market the following morning. The entire waterfront area near the market smelled like my dinner from the previous evening. Huge corrugated-metal smoking houses processed tons of bonito each year and the distinctive odor was everywhere. Skipjack tuna/Maldive fish is actually not tuna at all, but rather a type of bonito from the family *Scombridae*. It is caught by islanders using fishing poles and nearly all of the surplus fresh and sun-dried fish is brought to the Male central market. Maldive fish is cheap, readily available, and easy to buy in any quantity. It is a basic commodity in the Maldives. I wanted burlap bags full of the stuff and, as Don Tutu pointed out: "Maldive fish? Oh, yes . . . this where the action is."

Don showed me how to distinguish quality based on the size of fillet, the degree of dryness and/or smoke, the color, and the type of bonito; plus several ways that lower grades of dried fish could be made to look like a higher grade. As we talked to several dealers the thought occurred to me that if I traveled to the distant atolls, where most of the fishing was done, I could buy directly from the fishermen at a lower price than what was being quoted in the Male fish market. With this plan in mind, I decided to make a trip to one of the outer atolls. The only way to do this was on one of the small open-decked, interisland sailboats known as *dhonis*. Don Tutu taught me my first Dhivehi phrase: "Me dhoni dhanee kon-tan-aka?"—Where is this dhoni going?

If I succeeded in buying directly from the fishermen I planned to bring sacks of dried fish back to Male to stockpile in my bungalow at the Drummer's Shelter. When I had enough, I would book space on one of the small cargo boats that ply the black-market trade route to Sri Lanka. The Maldive fish trade was based on trust. I didn't know many people, but I figured that Don Tutu would be able to help me. Before any of this could happen, of course, I had to find good quality Maldive fish at a low price and get them back to Male.

I liked the thought of doing business directly with the remote island communities. From what Don told me, they had no local outlet for their surplus commodities, which consisted of woven mats, handmade coconut-fiber rope, dried coconut meat and Maldive fish. Everything the outer islanders produced or grew for sale had to be brought to the markets on Male where they had to compete with other islanders selling identical goods. I realized I could get a better price for Maldive fish on the islands, and that the fishermen would get more from me than they could hope for in the Male fish market. After discussing this plan with Don, I spent a few days changing money and buying barter goods, gifts and food. Don taught me a few basic Dhivehi phrases and my numbers. When I was ready, I found a dhoni and headed south with no particular atoll or island group in mind. I was gone for three weeks.

When I returned to the Drummer's Shelter I didn't have a single Maldive fish with me. Instead, I was sick with fever and vomiting uncontrollably. At dawn on my first day back I was panting for air as I lay naked on the cool concrete floor, pouring water over my body in an attempt to lower my temperature. By midday I was roasting in the furnacelike heat generated from the corrugated-metal roof of the bungalow. The cross-ventilation brought in wave after wave of saunalike heat. I waited a day hoping my fever and nausea would pass. But they didn't, and by the third day I knew that something was terribly wrong. I called out for Don Tutu to help me.

I was delirious with fever and I remember very little of the next few days apart from the dust, the stifling heat and the blinding light that made it excruciatingly painful to move my eyes. I literally had to crawl to the toilet on my hands and knees. Don Tutu's wife tried to get me to drink water from young coconuts, but I couldn't keep anything down. At the end of the fifth day I managed to get myself to the island health clinic, where I was diagnosed with hepatitis.

"Bad drinking water, or contaminated food, or close contact with an infected person," Dr. Rashid told me. He also said that, based on the blood test, I might suffer permanent liver damage. The only cure was complete rest.

"The people here want color televisions before they want clean drinking water," said Dr. Rashid. "No public health program and the people still dig shallow wells in the porous ground near the toilets. Hepatitis is spreading everywhere. It is a shame. And, oh . . . by the way, if you survive, would you like to rent an island? I can get you a good price."

I told him I would think about it.

As I lurched toward the door, he tried to reassure me by saying that with a case like mine only four out of ten people would die.

"Only four out of ten?" I croaked. "Oh, I feel so much better already." I collapsed on the floor and had to be taken back to the Drummer's Shelter on a stretcher carried by four young men.

For two weeks I lay on a bed in my bungalow with hardly enough strength to sit up. All I could keep down was fresh coconut water with lime juice. My eyes ached so badly that I had to turn my head to look to the side. I continued to lose weight rapidly as I baked in my tin-roofed cubicle. One day Don Tutu's wife found me unconscious on the floor of my room. I couldn't keep food in my stomach, and anything but small sips of tepid coconut water brought on waves of nausea. I vomited bile and blood and whatever else my stomach could expel. The mosquito net over the bed was full of holes and as I lay on a woven mat stained with my own sweat the sand flies and mosquitoes had a field day. I couldn't summon the energy to swat the insects, and when the delirium had finally passed I felt as if I had drifted to the edge of life. Only by concentrating on a distant inner sense of survival did I manage to bring myself back. The fever had driven me into a state of mind where I could not distinguish between the past and present.

For another month I had no strength. I rested and let my thoughts wander for hours. Random moments from my childhood came back to me: the smell of freshly mowed lawn, tree forts, learning to ride a bicycle, the first time I heard a northern mockingbird's song, and barefoot summers at my grandmother's house making peach ice cream in the shade of an old apricot tree. I wondered if I would ever see my family again.

Like my journey to the south in search of Maldive fish, everything else that happened to me before my illness seemed like a dream: memories from another life. It was now as if I had been reborn. The beauty of early morning sunlight slanting into the yard of the Drummer's Shelter brought tears to my eyes and when I was strong enough to lift a full bucket of water over my head I luxuriated in the simple pleasure of letting cool water slowly flow down my sides. It felt so good just to be alive. By the time I was out of danger Don Tutu confided that he had seen many people die of hepatitis and judging from the extent of my illness and my rapid decline, he had felt certain the disease would kill me.

After the worst was over, Don Tutu came to my room every morning and set a breakfast tray by my bed with a glass of fresh coconut water, lemon juice and glucose. Some days I took a bite of banana or a slice of ripe mango that I simply let melt in my mouth. It was all I could do to eat a bite of dry cracker or a spoonful of plain rice porridge. After the breakfast tray was taken away, Don came back to the room to practice his English. The session usually lasted no more than an hour because I was still so weak. I wasn't in the mood to talk, but he and his wife had taken care of me and I didn't want to refuse his simple request. We came to an agreement. In exchange for my correcting his English, he would tell me stories about his coming of age in the Maldives. As I got better, and his stories improved, Don's visits grew longer.

At first, I concentrated on his pronunciation, verb tense, and word choice, but within days I was intently writing down the stories as he spoke. He brought to life a traditional culture that was rapidly vanishing. We eventually narrowed the topic of conversation to common courtship practices in his youth. They included several highlights from his earliest sexual adventures.

"When I was a young man," Don Tutu told me one morning, "the girls used to tease the boys who were shy by calling out, 'Call-aye-ga la lee na-tee-tah?' It means—'Don't you have a penis?'"

If a young, unmarried man wanted to find a lover there were some young boys who acted as go-betweens. This was to help save face, but the go-betweens also knew the young women who might be interested. "We called it night fishing," said Don.

On Don's first night-fishing expedition, he was led to a bedroom window on a moonless night. He had no idea whose window he was knocking on. "Sometimes the girls were only thirteen or fourteen, but usually they were older and experienced," said Don. Following local custom, he stood at the closed window, knocked a few more times and when he heard a young woman's voice he said: "Good evening, I am Beru Don Tutu [his full name] and I am very pleased to meet you." In the Maldives people are very class conscious and your name identifies your social class and family. Don got lucky at his first window. The girl opened the shutters, Don climbed into her bed, and they made love in the dark. Don had no idea who he was having sex with while outside a couple of his friends and the go-between stood watch. The lookouts were not so much for the girl's relatives or her father as for other young men who might suddenly arrive for a bit of night fishing of their own at the same bedroom window.

According to Don Tutu, these nocturnal visits sometimes ended badly and he was forced to make several hasty escapes. This entailed jumping out the window with his clothes tucked under his arm, vaulting over the nearest coral-block wall, and then sprinting naked into the night. I recognized such episodes as a universal rite of passage experienced by young men worldwide. It brought back memories of my own teenage years in California in the mid-1960s.

Lookouts were also important because if another man came along unexpectedly and caught someone in bed with one of his regular girls there was a traditional form of revenge. The jealous party would conceal himself in the bushes until the other man was leaving, then throw a half-coconut shell full of urine all over him. Sometimes there were fights between suitors and, in the quiet village setting, the cause of the commotion was clear to everyone within hearing distance.

The father of a sexually active girl would usually keep quiet and be patient unless too many men were making visits to her window. Once the neighbors or other family members started to talk it was time for the father to take action in order to avoid bringing shame on the family. The father would generally suggest to his daughter that she should select the one she loved the most and try to marry him. Most parents had engaged in night-fishing expeditions of their own during their youth, so when their children came of age, the parents knew how to respond in a way which was rarely angry or hurtful.

"How could this have been so acceptable, especially in a Muslim community?" I asked.

"Muslim? Christian? Buddha people? All the same. We were young people. It is nature!" Don said.

When I asked Don if the go-betweens or the girls ever asked for money, he said, "Oh, my goodness . . . no! They never ask for money. It would be shameful to ask for money. It would make them like prostitutes."

"And illegitimate children?" I asked.

"In those days things very wild," said Don. "Always marrying and getting divorced. No one can keep track of who is legitimate and who isn't. Eighty, maybe ninety percent divorce rate. Very wild living, I tell you. You get my meaning? Not like today. Oh, no. Now everyone very civilized! Night fishing still happen I think, but now everybody not talking."

Don talked about many things during our visits. In his lifetime, he could remember six murders and two suicides, but no rape. Thinking back, he did recall one incident: "Yes, when my grandfather was young there was a group of boys that got one young girl. They raped her and killed her. Terrible thing. Afterward they throw the body in the sea. Just like that. But that was before I born. So you see rape is not one of our customs.

"And we had punishments," Don said. "Drunk in public you get banishment to an outer island for one year plus forty strokes with wooden paddle to the back of the thighs. Very painful. Murder—banishment and one hundred strokes.

Adultery—one hundred strokes for the man and the same for the woman. Homosexuality—thirty-nine strokes."

"Thirty-nine? That is an unusual number," I said. "Why thirty-nine strokes for homosexuality?"

"Maybe because it a smaller crime than public drunkeness," Don suggested.

During the sultan's time, punishment for political crimes or violations of class taboos involved public canings. Eight men would hold the offending person facedown on the beach as two men with long-handled rattan canes took turns striking the blows one after the other. The name of the punishment was *booree hang naygong,* which in Dhivehi means "taking the skin from the back." Usually fifteen blows.

On days that I was feeling well enough, we would have our English lesson at Don's bungalow. One of the few sweet-water wells on the island was situated in the central courtyard of the Drummer's Shelter and every day young women and older girls from the neighborhood came to fill their brightly colored plastic buckets with water. Don told his stories while the two of us sat on a wide swinging seat suspended by coconut-fiber rope from the rafters of his front porch. The swing overlooked the well and one day I had a large bag of lemons that Don bought for me at the public market.

Two girls laughed at me as they walked by with buckets of water balanced on their heads. I asked Don what was so funny. "There is an old Maldivian wives' tale," he said. "Men who drink too much lemon juice cannot make proper erection. Even today women say to their husbands, 'Do not eat too many lemons or other sour food.' The girls are laughing because you have the big bag of lemons. You eat those lemons . . . you get no action. You get my meaning?"

We watched the activity at the well. The women liked Don and they tolerated his risqué comments. They laughed at his off-color suggestions and they were not timid to respond in kind. They made eyes at him and flirted openly. The flirting was a small kindness to an old man, but I also suspect that they kept up the banter because they needed his water. Apart from cigar smoking and conversation there were few pleasures left for Don Tutu. It was obvious from our afternoon visits by the well that he looked forward to these sessions on the porch.

The girls' banter sometimes made Don pensive and remote. It took him a while to confide in me. His wife was not yet thirty-five and he had married her as partial settlement for a complicated family debt that I never fully understood. He told me that her age made him sad because he could no longer make love to her. "And what is the point of having a young wife if you cannot please her?" he said.

"No erection at your age? It is nature," I said.

The women at the well had long black hair, large eyes, and nicely shaped figures. Long-sleeved smocks came down to their knees and covered loose-fitting pants. The women were slender, and fit, and after my long convalescence I enjoyed those afternoons by the well. One day the sight of the women at work brought back the memory of something that happened to me during my three-week journey to look for Maldive fish. Don Tutu and I were sitting on the swing seat when I asked him to translate a phrase that a young woman recited to me nearly two months earlier. I had met her on an island to the south. I read the Dhivehi words from my notebook, and Don Tutu listened with growing interest as the meaning became clear. The women at the well overheard the phrase. They giggled to themselves and covered their mouths with their hands. Don said something to them and one woman slapped another one on the back, bent over double and laughed until she cried.

"Ha!" Don Tutu exclaimed. "What the woman told you to write is this: 'If you do not come close to me soon, then I will come close to you.' I think maybe you already get her meaning, no? It is a very sweet thing for a young woman to say to a man. Did she ask for money?"

"No, money had nothing to do with it," I said.

"And was she beautiful?" Don Tutu asked.

"As beautiful as the women at your well," I said.

Overhead, the coconut-fiber ropes creaked gently as we continued to swing back and forth. Don's wife brought us fresh coconut water in glasses. I took a sip, and once again the memories of Nahimah came back to me. I could still remember the sound of her voice, the scent of her skin and the soft touch of her fingertips on my mouth.

"Well . . . come on. Who was she?" Don asked as he nudged my knee with the back of his hand. I settled into the cushions and told him the story.

I met Nahimah during my Maldive fish-buying expedition. The details from that time seemed unreal in the retelling, but I knew the events were not the product of my fever dreams. The day I left the Drummer's Shelter I joined four men who were returning to their island in South Male Atoll. It was midmorning when the boatman cast off the bowline at the main wharf by the Male fish market. He poled his twenty-five-foot-long, lanteen-rigged dhoni through a gap in the concrete-and-coral breakwater, and before long a sea breeze filled the sail and carried us into deep blue water. I wasn't sure where we were going and at the time I only knew a few phrases of Dhivehi. But it was a beautiful afternoon with a light wind blowing and scattered clouds that provided some shade. The sea was calm, flying fish skimmed across our bow and I was content to enjoy the journey without much conversation or knowledge of our exact destination. I figured any island we went to would have Maldive fish.

Before Male disappeared in our wake we were overtaken by a sudden squall that pelted the open deck and soaked us with warm rain and stinging salt-sea spray. The sky cleared and we slowly dried off in the midday sun. A short while later a rope broke and the sail and boom fell off the mast hitting the man next to me on the head, knocking him unconscious. No sooner had the man come to his senses than the rudder fell to pieces. We drifted toward the open sea until the boatman constructed a makeshift rudder replacement from a loose floorboard, and then rerigged the sail. The other passengers showed no outward signs that any of these events were out of the ordinary. They seemed to have total confidence in the boatman's ability to keep the dhoni afloat and on course. Their trust was rewarded, and we continued sailing due south without any further problems.

We followed a line of low, coconut-palm-covered islands. These were but a small sampling of the more than one thousand coral islands in the Maldives. I remembered the colors and described them to Don. Dark green coconut palms; white sand beaches; aquamarine and turquoise lagoons; and the deep blue-black of the bottomless sea. Islands appeared and disappeared as we moved along. I saw men loading their anchored boats with blocks of coral, saw the Male fishing fleet and a few other dhonis, like ours, moving between the islands. Some dhonis carried a small headsail, and the booms and mainsails on the lanteen rigs were all bent into beautiful shapes with the uppermost tip of the sail occasionally vibrating under the pressure of the wind. The sun was hot that day. I took a long sip from my water bottle and then curled up for a siesta in the shade of my large black umbrella, which was nearly four feet wide.

Hours passed and when I awoke we were approaching a small, parklike island shaded by closely planted coconut palms. The helmsman brought the boat about, and we sailed through a narrow opening in the barrier reef. As we entered the placid lagoon the water once again changed from dark blue to turquoise. The bow of the dhoni nudged the broken-coral and sand beach, and only when we came to a stop did I realize how hot it was.

At first glance, the island seemed deserted as the men collected their few belongings and jumped off the bow and waded ashore. They motioned me to follow them and as I moved toward the line of palm trees, the dry, coarse sand felt good as it crunched beneath my bare feet. They indicated that we would unload my boxes of food and trade goods later. A band of naked children ran through the shade of the trees and a cool salt-sea breeze blew at our backs from the lagoon behind us.

I saw women at work, dressed in knee-length smocks over

long loose pants, or bare-shouldered with lengths of floral-print fabric tied above their breasts and extending to just below their knees. Many of the women were bent double as they swept the sand between the palm trees with short-handled twig brooms. The main pathways through the village and the open areas between the single-story houses were covered with delicate, fan-shaped patterns left by the brooms. Far in the distance waves crashed on the barrier reef as I carried my bag further into the shade. A few pieces of corrugated metal could be seen on the rooftops of the coral-block houses, but many of the roofs were of palm thatch. I didn't see one electrical wire, windowpane, padlock or pair of shoes. Everyone was barefoot or wearing rubber thongs. Doors were left open and there was a blessed lack of mechanical noise. Somewhere in the distance a radio played "If I Were a Rich Man" from *Fiddler on the Roof.* It was much cooler in the shade and a feeling of serenity prevailed.

The boatman left me at the headman's house. Mr. Suleiman was not home, but his wife showed me to the living room and storage area filled with sacks of what smelled like Maldive fish. Set flush into the concrete floor of the room was an old television picture tube. The gray-green rectangle of thick glass looked like a gigantic floor tile. Mrs. Suleiman brought me a cup of sweet black tea with a small plate of fried and salted breadfruit chips before returning to her work.

The island appeared to be populated only by women and children, but I learned through Mrs. Suleiman's gestures that her husband and most of the men were out on the fishing boats. They would return after sunset. Leaving my bag next to the television tube, I went outside and sat on a wood-framed, woven-rope cot in the shade of a coconut palm. Three little boys approached to within twenty feet of me, but they were hesitant to come any closer. I made a paper airplane, threw it to them, and when they brought it back to me I handed them pieces of paper to show them how to fold the wings. Before long, the ground was littered with the wreckage of little paper planes. I pretended to be a gorilla and slowly chased the boys through the trees. When they eventually grew tired of paper airplanes and a lumbering, snarling white man the boys went off to play with their miniature dhonis in the shallows and I settled in for an afternoon nap.

That evening I ate by myself, a simple dinner of fried Maldive fish and rice prepared by Mrs. Suleiman. An hour after nightfall the men returned. I met Mr. Suleiman, but because we had no language in common our communication was limited to the basics. He spoke to me in Dhivehi, while I spoke a few memorized phrases that Don Tutu had taught me, and somehow we came to an understanding. I indicated that I was interested in staying on the island to visit. For his part, Mr. Suleiman made it clear that I was his guest and that I could stay as long as I wanted. I attempted to explain that I was willing to pay something for staying in his home, and that I had brought food, but even had I been fluent in his language, the concept of a paying guest was beyond his understanding. There were plenty of cots to sleep on, the fish came from the sea, the fruit from the trees . . . and who would dream of charging a stranger from a distant land for rice or the occasional cup of tea? He went to eat his dinner and left me to myself.

A short time passed before a group of neighbors came to

look at me. We nodded and smiled at one another and I stood up as men came forward to shake my hand. The children chattered and there was a considerable amount of whispering, but everyone seemed friendly as I introduced myself. A few people repeated my name. Having satisfied their curiosity, everyone left the room. By early evening I was stretched out on a cot reading by the light of a single kerosene wick stuck into the top of a tin can. Glancing up from the page I saw a girl standing in the open doorway watching me. I was reading Henry Miller. I smiled to the girl then went back to a passage describing life in America.

> We moved in a swarm, intent on accomplishing one thing—to make life easy . . . there was only a wilderness of steel and iron, of stocks and bonds, of crops and produce, of factories, mills and lumber yards . . . as many times as I struck out to scour the land, I always came back empty-handed. Nothing new, nothing bizarre, nothing exotic . . . only a wilderness of boredom, of useless utilities, of loveless love.

Finishing the passage, I looked up and saw a young man. His bare upper body and head were framed by an opened window. He stared at me, looked at my book, and then shifted his attention to the girl. She couldn't have been much older than fourteen. Their eyes met. They exchanged a knowing look, the girl giggled, and then the two of them ran off in the direction of the darkened beach. The book seemed a lot less interesting after that.

I snuffed out the wick and tried to sleep, but the airless

coral-block room was too humid and full of mosquitoes for me to get comfortable. The stinking sacks of dried Maldive fish that were piled high along one wall didn't help, but I made a mental note to see if I could buy a few sacks to take back to Male. I moved my pillow and bedsheet to the outdoor cot where I had taken my nap that afternoon. I lit a mosquito coil and placed it beneath the cot, then lay down and pulled the sheet over my head. I fell asleep listening to the rustling of palm fronds overhead, and during the night woke up several times to hear the reassuring sound of breakers pounding the distant reef.

The next morning the men left in the boats before first light. I didn't hear them go, but they must have walked right past me as I slept, because at first light I could see a line of fresh footprints that passed by my cot and led to the beach. After a cup of sweet black tea and a plate of cold Maldive fish and rice, I gave Mr. Suleiman's wife a small box full of food and gifts I had brought with me. The box contained unimaginable luxuries from distant ports of call. Things like: bars of Camay bath soap, bottles of liquid hair shampoo, a hand mirror, needles, tinned chicken curries from Indonesia, powdered milk from Australia, a sack of rice, ballpoint pens, packets of double-edged razor blades, tubes of lipstick and a large tin of cream-filled cookies from Singapore. The biggest hit with Mrs. Suleiman, apart from the cookies, was an assortment of large hair clips with big plastic flowers.

I explored the island. It was about four hundred yards long and one hundred fifty yards wide. I estimated the highest vantage point to be about thirty-six inches above sea level. A winding footpath led to a second village on the island's northern end. Each village had its own separate beach and fleet of fishing boats, and the people from the two communities seemed to keep to their own side of the island.

Near the beach on Mr. Suleiman's side of the island I came upon a group of older men and their young apprentices who were working on a new dhoni. In the shade of a thatch-roofed hut without walls the men were planing hull planks and carving hardwood dowels by hand. All the work was done sitting or kneeling on the sand. I watched for a while, but there was no way to talk and when I grew tired of watching them work I moved on.

As I walked by a row of huts a man called out in broken English to invite me to sit with him on his front porch, where he was keeping his son company. The little boy lay on his back on a raised bed. His lap was covered by a draped piece of fabric which was hung from a rafter on a length of string. The boy had just been circumcised and the fabric cover was set up to prevent chafing and to keep the flies away until the wound healed. Adam Foulou, the man who had called to me, was one of two circumcision masters on the island. He spoke English from his days as a laborer on the recently abandoned British naval base far to the south on Gan Island in Addu Atoll. He talked about the fine art of circumcision and to show me examples of his work he called three boys to come join us. They lined up in a row and Mr. Foulou asked them to lift their sarongs so I could look at their penises. They did so without any sign of hesitation or embarrassment. I examined the row of little boys and their tiny circumcised penises, then nodded my head in approval. The boys dropped the hems of their sarongs and went back to their game.

Mr. Foulou explained how the operation was performed, with a straight razor and no anesthetic. Before making the cut, however, it was customary to first apply the juice of a red onion to the end of the penis. This was to keep it flaccid and facilitate the work. When Adam Foulou was not working on foreskins he pursued his normal occupation as the island blacksmith. In his front yard he had set up an anvil, a hand-cranked blower, an assortment of sledgehammers, and several gunny sacks full of charcoal. He specialized in pounding shallow cooking pots from sections of discarded oil drums, but he also forged handsome coconut cleavers from car leaf springs. Judging from the circumcised penises and the pounded oil-drum pots, he was a meticulous craftsman. He dried fish as a sideline and I bought my first sack of Maldive fish from Mr. Foulou.

While I was dozing on my cot that afternoon a little boy brought me a green coconut. He expertly cleaved off the top with a heavy blade then offered me the cool drink. "Nama kee ko bah? [What is the name of this?]" I asked, pointing first at the coconut, then the knife. He told me, and I added the two new words to my list of Dhivehi. More boys gathered, first to watch, then to offer their own words in exchange for the English equivalent. Each child memorized his own word so that when I pointed to him he would reply by saying "seashell," "flower," "belly button," "tree," "big toe" or whatever word he had originally chosen. During the afternoon work break thirty or forty women and older girls gathered around my cot where I was still writing down words and practicing my pronunciation with the boys. My attempts to speak the language were well received, and everyone was fascinated with how I could write down letters that matched the sounds of their words. During the language lesson a young woman sat down beside me. I had never seen her before and she was very pretty.

"Nama kee ko bah?" she asked, pointing to my pen.

"Pen," I said.

"Pen," she repeated.

"Nama kee ko bah?" she continued, this time pointing to her eyes.

"Eyes," I replied, taking a good look at hers.

"Low," she said, giving me the Dhivehi word.

Others wanted to know the words for head, ear, nose and foot. We were making our way through the common body parts when, without warning, one of the smallest boys let out a tremendous fart. On cue, a coconut fell from a palm as if the shock waves from the fart had dislodged it. Conversation stopped as everyone looked at the boy. It seemed impossible that such a small child could have produced such an enormous sound, but judging from his own expression of astonishment there could be little doubt that he was the one. Everyone erupted in laughter. The incident made everyone relax and at the same time it created a new line of vocabulary words.

"Nama kee ko bah?" an older woman laughed, gesturing toward the child.

"Fart," I answered.

"Furt?" the woman said tentatively. I repeated the word and others joined in with a chorus of "ferts," "forts," "firts" before they got it right. The older women exchanged whispers and then they urged the young woman at my side to ask for other words. She put her hand on her thigh and asked for the word in English. We moved on to her hips and stomach and by the time we had worked our way up to her breasts my interest in the language had risen considerably. Catching the drift of the conversation, a little boy moved toward a group of pubescent girls and with his index finger he pressed gently on a budding breast. He rubbed the girl's nipple in a circular motion and told me the name in Dhivehi. The girl responded with a simple nod, as if to say, "Yes, that is the correct word."

Before long the women were asking about the size of families in America. Women in the Maldives average five or six children each and so naturally they wanted to know about condoms and birth control pills. When I realized what they were asking I immediately remembered the sign at the airport prohibiting the import of Buddha images and condoms. The women's questions were conveyed with straightforward gestures and pantomime that left nothing to the imagination. At one point the conversation turned to breast-feeding and as part of a woman's explanation she pulled up her blouse to show me her breasts. She took a nipple in her fingers and pointed toward the baby in her lap. They wanted to know if American women had their babies at home or in the "clinic." It was at about this point in the conversation that I began wondering what the men might think if they knew how the language lesson was progressing. After more than an hour of talk the women returned to their homes to resweep the neighborhood pathways and prepare dinner. As they walked away I could hear them practicing new words such as "ko ko nat" . . . "my foot" . . . and "nipple." Based on my previous visits to other Islamic countries, where women are routinely veiled, I found it difficult to believe how relaxed and open and natural these women had been with me. When the young woman next to me stood up to leave she pointed to herself and said, "Nahimah."

"Eric," I replied, touching my hand to my chest.

"Ar-eek," she said. Nahimah walked off slowly. I watched her until she was out of sight. She looked back once.

The story of the language lesson must have circulated that evening because an hour after the boats returned four young men came into my room at Mr. Suleiman's house, where I had just settled on a price for a second bag of Maldive fish. One man poked at me with his hand to get my attention. Then he made a crossed-finger sign with his two index fingers that I didn't understand. But I had a sense that the gesture had something to do with my talk with the women that afternoon.

I didn't want to make myself unwelcome so soon after arriving on the island and the next day I went out on the boats to make friends with the men and see how they caught Maldive fish. Well before first light, the open boat was at sea and I was shivering in the bottom of a stinking dhoni, trying to keep myself warm by the heat of a single clove cigarette that I held in my hand. The men started catching fish with poles and baited hooks. The hooked fish seemed to fall from the sky from every direction, and the bottom of the boat began to fill. Midmorning, we took a break for a bite to eat. More Maldive fish and cold rice. Several of the men knew a few English words and expressions, but the men in my boat were loud and tactless. "Hallo my darling!" was a phrase they never seemed to tire of, and even among themselves a sense of bravado dominated their conversations. They blurted out questions for each other's enjoyment, but seldom waited for a response from me. By midday I was knee-deep in dead fish, sunburned and thirsty. I couldn't wait to get back to the island.

Late in the day a forty-foot-long Japanese fishing boat pulled alongside and tied up to the dhoni. The two Japanese crewmen paid no attention to me as the fish were off-loaded. The Japanese boat would later transfer the catch to a mother ship where the fish were processed. At dusk we were motoring back to the island. Sitting in the bottom of the boat I didn't mind the stink of the fish oil, or the uneasy roll of the boat, but the endless guffawing and smirking of my fellow shipmates convinced me not to come out on the boats again. "Hallo my darling! . . . Hallo my darling!" they yelled maniacally. When we finally reached the island, I thanked them, accepted a few stiffened, sunbaked fish as a gift and then said, "Good-bye my darlings!"

"Good-bye my darlings," they shouted back.

For the next week, the days passed pleasantly. I bought a third sack of Maldive fish from Mr. Suleiman, and Nahimah came to visit me every afternoon. I wrote down Dhivehi words and she managed to memorize English terms quickly. It didn't take long before I found myself getting restless in anticipation of our afternoon language lesson. I managed to maintain the assumption that her primary interest was learning English, until the day two of her girlfriends joined us where we sat on my cot beneath the palm trees. One of the girls pointed at me, then at Nahimah. She crossed her two index fingers. Right over left, then left over right. It was the same gesture the four men had made in Mr. Suleiman's house my second night on the island. When I didn't catch the meaning the girl gently patted Nahimah on the stomach before repeating the sign with her fingers. To make certain I understood, she again pointed at me then formed an imaginary swollen tummy on Nahimah. The message was becoming more clear.

The three of them laughed in such a natural, innocent and uncomplicated way that all I could do was laugh with them. Their open and uninhibited behavior had me confused because, after all, this was a Muslim community. Nahimah's gaze met mine and at that precise moment I began to wonder what it would feel like to be dismembered by island men wielding Mr. Foulou's leaf-spring coconut cleavers.

Thursday afternoon, the day before the Muslim holy day, the fishing boats were hauled out of the water. Heavy coconut-fiber ropes were attached to the bows and a single set of evenly spaced log rollers led to the top of the slightly inclined beach. As the bow of the first boat was being positioned at the log nearest the water's edge the women gestured for me to come help them pull on the ropes. The men were slightly amused that I would take part in woman's work, but as a stranger I was free to do as I pleased. The men held the boat level, and as we all began pulling I became aware of a pair of firm breasts beneath a wet blouse rubbing against the back of my hands. Another pair were soon felt pressing against my shoulder. I realized this was no coincidence when I looked at the expressions on the women's faces. While they were enjoying their little joke I continued to pull on the rope, thinking how woman's work wasn't such a humiliating task after all.

After a week of language lessons with Nahimah I had enough common words so that I could express simple ideas from memorized phrases. This allowed me to visit the people from both sides of the island more freely. Mr. Foulou sometimes came along to translate for me. I spent most of my mornings with the children and the boatbuilders. Midday was for reading or snorkeling along the edge of the reef where, on one occasion, I was surrounded by a school of dolphins that emitted high-pitched squeaking sounds before swimming away. By midafternoon I would start thinking about Nahimah. The language lessons continued, usually just between Nahimah and myself, and it was during one of these meetings on my cot that she had me write down a phrase of several lines. She took great care that I get it right. This was the phrase that I later read to Don Tutu on the swing seat at the Drummer's Shelter.

As Nahimah went over each word I couldn't be sure of the literal translation, but from the look in her eyes I pretty well caught the meaning. Nahimah was unmarried and probably sixteen or seventeen years old. I was ten years older. She was asking me to have sex with her. I knew what I wanted to do, but if I responded, I wondered what this would mean? I carefully considered the consequences of what I might be getting myself into. The moral and ethical debate raged in my mind for approximately one second before I made the crossed-finger sign, pointed to both of us and nodded *aan* (yes). Pleased with herself, Nahimah stood up, smiled, and then walked home.

A day of uncertainty went by before I settled on a plan. After my ten days on the island I was familiar with people's movements. In the evenings it was customary to visit other households after dinner. An hour or so later everyone would return to their own homes. It was at this time, when people were moving about the village, that I started taking walks to an isolated beach at the northern end of the island. The beach was only a couple of hundred yards from the village, but bushes grew thickly at the top of the sand, creating little secluded pockets of sand visible only from the lagoon. Based on my observations, I figured this was the place where couples went for their night-fishing rendezvous.

The beach was about a five-minute walk in the dark through a maze of coconut palms. Like all of my other habits, I knew it wouldn't take long before my evening walks were noticed. I hoped that Nahimah would notice, or that this information would be passed on to her. I waited on the beach for two nights with no results. Both evenings I thought I saw movement at the far end of the beach, but even in the faint moonlight I could not be sure. On the third night I saw a figure step from the coconut palms and then move along the edge of the water in my direction. I recognized the walk and the silhouette. It was Nahimah. I got up and walked toward her until we were facing each other on the sand. We stood close without speaking until Nahimah reached up and lightly brushed my lips with her fingertips.

"Nama kee ko bah?" she whispered.

"Thunfaiy," I replied. She withdrew her hand without taking her eyes from mine.

"Nama kee ko bah?" she asked, touching the nape of her neck.

"Karu," I said.

Even before I put my mouth to her neck I knew I was lost. The taste of her mouth and the fragrance of her skin and hair were from another world. She put my hand to her breast.

"Nama kee ko bah?" she asked again, more softly.

I couldn't remember the word but it didn't matter because there was nothing more to say. Without further guidance or vocabulary words I found the bottom hem to her knee-length smock, and some time later the top of her pants. The language lesson was over. Now, as we lay down on the dry sand, the sound of our breathing was enough to convey the important messages. Any hesitation or caution I may have entertained up to that point was abandoned the moment her bare stomach came up to meet mine. Half-dressed, we made love on the beach bathed in the hot night air. Seawater rushed onto the sand, and I was transported to a place where sex was pure and innocent, and natural and uncomplicated. God knows what Nahimah was thinking.

We made love for no more than twenty minutes and then Nahimah had to go. She stepped into her pants, pulled down her smock, smoothed it, and then walked back the way she had come. She disappeared into the wall of palm trees and I sat on the beach for a long time contemplating the deep set of knee and elbow prints in the sand. Nahimah's sweet, intimate fragrance lingered on my face and hands. I tossed my tangled sarong and T-shirt to one side and went for a swim in the lagoon. I swam away from the beach for about five minutes and then floated on my back looking up at the night sky. The water was warm, and from offshore no lights were showing on the island.

I returned to the beach, where I dressed and then smoothed

the sand to remove all traces of where we had made love. But it became obvious to me that the two sets of different-sized footprints leading to the patch of disturbed sand would clearly tell the story to any islander who walked by before the next high tide. My large footprints were unmistakable. I walked back to my cot in a trance, fell asleep with my heart still pounding, and didn't wake until after sunrise.

That day the language lessons continued as usual on the cot. Nahimah was wearing a large hair clip with a red plastic hibiscus which Mrs. Suleiman must have given her. Going over our words and phrases, I tried to detect some obvious signs of change in Nahimah's behavior toward me, but there were none. Looking at her, I found it hard to believe I hadn't imagined the previous night on the beach, but my lingering erotic state and Nahimah's aloof manner merely added to my desire. I longed to know her thoughts, and to make love with her again, but she did not provide me with a tangible clue of any sort that anything out of the ordinary had passed between us.

A storm approached the island. We fell silent as we looked out to sea. A double-masted *batelee,* under full sail, was running before the wind. It moved quickly through the water in the direction of the island, with taut, white canvas sails dramatically set against a towering wall of black clouds that filled the southern sky. The sun disappeared and an uneasy calm fell over the surface of the sea. Moments later, when the wind began to pick up, an eerie blue-black shadow spread over the island. Day was transformed into dusk and the boat, unable to outrun the storm, dropped its lanteen sails just as it was engulfed by the immense wall of dark clouds. The first blast of wind reached the island bringing down a shower of dead palm fronds and coconuts. The palms bent away from the direction of the storm then swayed violently from side to side in the confused blast of winds. The downpour was sudden and powerful, but it lasted no more than fifteen minutes. Rather than running for shelter, Nahimah and I sat on the cot and pulled up our feet as I opened my umbrella. With her back to me, I wrapped my legs around her and pulled her close with my arms. Huge raindrops pounded the top of the umbrella and we were bathed in a fine warm mist. The village was cut off from view by the sheets of driving rain as we huddled against each other. It was as if we were riding out the storm in a very small boat. Nahimah felt soft and warm and once again I caught the sweet scent of her skin. It was like nutmeg or cloves and I found it hard to believe that someone who lived on a regular diet of Maldive fish could smell so good. By the time the rain let up we had moved apart. The sun was low on the horizon and the sailboat was entering the lagoon. When Nahimah got up to return to her father's house she looked at me, leaned forward to where I was sitting at the edge of the cot and once again lightly touched my lips with her fingertips as I kissed them. It was the last time we were alone together and the last time we touched. That night she did not come to the beach.

The sailboat had brought a traveling doctor who was making a tour of the remote islands. He had trained in Bangalore, India, and spoke English fluently. That night at Mr. Suleiman's house he told me he was visiting the outer islands to search for new cases of leprosy, which often go undetected and which can be transmitted before there is any outward sign of the disease. The next morning the doctor held an open-air clinic to treat minor wounds and instruct people on basic hygiene. He also handed out medicine. The doctor was leaving that afternoon and he invited me to join him on his rounds. His next destinations were the leper colonies on the nearby islands of Biadu and Vilinggilli Varu. Assuring me the inhabitants were not contagious, he promised to bring me back to the island in four or five days. I left my three burlap sacks of dried fish at Mr. Suleiman's house and let him know I would be back soon.

A large crowd of women and children came to the beach to see us off and I asked the doctor to explain I would be returning in a few days. I had him mention that I would be coming back to buy more sacks of Maldive fish, but this was simply my way of letting Nahimah know my plans. She stood in the crowd looking shy and at ease, and I found it difficult not to stare at her. I assumed that her friends knew about our meeting on the beach, but there was no sign of this. Nahimah joined the others at the water's edge as they waved good-bye. I waved back. The sails were raised and the boat heeled slightly as it moved toward the entrance of the lagoon. I sat amidships, looking at the people on the beach until I could no longer distinguish Nahimah from the others.

The hospital boat sailed out of the lagoon headed for Biadu Island where we spent the night. Two days later I came down with a fever. I couldn't eat or drink and I vomited until I thought I would bring up my stomach. When the doctor noticed the whites of my eyes turning yellow he ordered the boat back to Male, where I managed to get to the Drummer's Shelter before I collapsed.

"So, that is the story of where I went and about the girl who gave me the sentence," I told Don.

"Will you go back to the island?" he asked.

"I don't think so," I said.

I closed my notebook that held Nahimah's phrase and, for the first time, I accepted the fact that I would never see her again. I didn't return to the island, although I thought about it frequently during my last month at the Drummer's Shelter. I told myself that too much time had passed for me to return, but I knew that this was merely my way of preserving what I considered to be a perfect moment in time. I preferred the memory of making love to a beautiful stranger on a warm sand beach to the reality of going back to the island. And what about Nahimah? Had I already compromised her future? Or maybe, as Don Tutu had already told me, it was still an acceptable custom for young women and men to satisfy their sexual curiosity. When I explained my conflicted thoughts to Don Tutu, he merely let out a laugh and said, "You are young people. And these feelings? It is nature!"

I eventually regained my health. At the Male fish market I bought fifteen burlap sacks of Maldive fish and made arrangements to take them with me on a small cargo boat. I said good-bye to Don Tutu and his wife and thanked them for taking care of me and for the hospitality and friendship and stories. By the time I reached the wharf that night, the boat was loaded and the deckhand ready to cast off the lines. I climbed aboard. The engine rumbled to life and beneath a star-filled sky we moved into deep water, bound for Galle Harbor on the southwest coast of Sri Lanka.

Long after I left the Maldives, fragments of Dhivehi sometimes came back to me at unexpected moments. I returned to the United States and for years I could remember the sounds of words and phrases that had lost their meanings. But now, even the sounds have left me and I have forgotten nearly everything. Everything, that is, except the sweet memory of night fishing with Nahimah.

LIFE LESSONS FROM DYING
STRANGERS

IN THE SPRING of 1977 I decided to send two large steamer trunks and a wooden packing crate from Calcutta to San Francisco. Looking at the original shipping manifest, I can see there were Buddhist prayer flags, a Tibetan wool robe, a finely made traditional chopstick and knife set, and a half-dozen mismatched English tea cups and saucers that I collected during a six-hundred-mile walk along the Tibet/Nepal border. There was also a maroon-colored, handmade waxed cotton umbrella with split-bamboo splines that I acquired from a Buddhist monk near the Temple of the Tooth in Sri Lanka in exchange for a tube of toothpaste. One trunk was filled with an assortment of nineteenth-century jewelry-making dies from Sikkim, a dozen Afghan turbans from Mazār-i-Sharīf, a complete set of cast-bronze antique opium weights from Mandalay, hundreds of matchbook covers, and a cast-aluminum nutcracker in the shape of a woman's hips and legs. My most coveted possession was a six-foot by ten-foot hand-painted canvas Hindi movie poster of the actor Robin Bannerjee serenading three gorillas of unknown gender and an overweight woman clad in leopard skins in the 1950s Hindi movie version of *Tarzan*. The other trunk contained first editions of Henry Miller (sold from under the counter as pornography, from a secondhand book dealer in Calcutta), kilos of cardamom pods and cloves, South Indian cookbooks and fragrant rosewood that, in log form, had been carried across a Calcutta lumber-yard, by an elephant, to a gigantic band saw where a crew of laborers reduced it to rough-cut planks. Each of my trunks when filled to capacity weighed more than two hundred pounds and I kept them beside my bed at the Salvation Army Hostel on Sudder Street.

As I looked into the different shipping possibilities, I con-tinued to collect more items. Hand-pulled rickshaws arrived at the front gate of the hotel with cartons of sandalwood soap, Indian cooking utensils, a hand-powered jeweler's-wire rolling mill, a collection of metal and wood antique locks from Northern Pakistan and Nepal, and a disassembled turned-wood chair from the mountains of Nuristan, a remote region of Afghanistan located north of the Khyber Pass. When I realized I couldn't fit everything into the steamer trunks I ordered timber for the construction of a large shipping crate. I summoned two carpenters from New Bazaar. We agreed on a price and the men set to work in the hotel courtyard. They squatted on the paving stones and sawed and hammered rough-cut planks into a sturdy shipping crate. There was a surcharge to cover the cost of recycled nails, a small fee for coconut oil to lubricate the saws, plus a resharpening fee for the wood block plane and the two handsaws.

When the carpenters were finished they sold the offcuts and sawdust to the pavement dwellers who lived along Sudder

Street. These street people, in turn, resold the solid bits of wood for a small profit. They kept the sawdust to mix with water and fresh cow dung from the street which was then mixed into stiff, moist patties and slapped onto the walls of a nearby building to dry in the sun. When they started to peel off the walls the patties were used as fuel for cooking fires on the sidewalk.

During the first week of my stay in Calcutta the hotel manager seemed to take scant interest in my activities, but by the middle of the second week he let it be known in the kindest sort of way that his hotel courtyard was not an open-air woodworking shop, nor was my room a storage shed.

In Calcutta, packages weighing less than twenty kilograms (with a circumference of no more than one meter and eighty centimeters) could be sent by regular mail provided the shipper has gone to the Tourist Office and obtained a Certificate of Gift Parcel. In front of most post offices in India there were men who, for a few rupees, would stitch unbleached muslin cloth around your gift parcel, then seal the seams with dabs of melted red wax for security. If it was necessary to itemize the contents for insurance or customs purposes, there were other men on the sidewalk with manual typewriters who would bang out a list in the shade of a tree while you waited. Fresh coconut juice vendors were set up nearby to provide customers with something cool to drink as the typists did their job. Light snacks were also available.

One day while I was walking myself, step-by-step, through the procedures for preparing parcels for the post office, I was approached by a man selling small rolled-up paper cones filled with toasted chickpeas and lentils mixed with minced onion, chopped green chilies, and salt with a squeeze of lime. I bought a cone and while I ate the warm, spicy mixture I started reading the printing on the paper cone. It was in English. The lines sounded familiar, but the cone was too tightly wrapped for me to identify the author. Most street food in India is wrapped in banana leaves or recycled paper ranging from Chinese pictorial magazines and Soviet-era soya-bean production worksheets to pages from English novels, high school exams, and—if you are really lucky—personal letters. When I finished my snack I unrolled the paper cone to discover a page from Shakespeare. It was *Henry IV, Part I*. I read a conversation between Falstaff and Prince Hal before wiping my fingers on the page and then placing the greasy, crumpled literature in a trash bin.

Once inside the post office, with the stitched and wax-sealed gift parcel in hand, it was necessary to determine which line to stand in. The lines of customers were long and slow and it was not unusual to wait an hour or more before reaching a clerk who might politely inform you that you were in the wrong line. Stamps would eventually be purchased at one window and insurance obtained from a second window. A third line led to a postal employee who placed a postmark on the stamps that you had purchased from one of the previous clerks, before the final act of mailing could be completed at a fourth window. The entire process could take hours and sometimes days, but this sort of express mail service was only for gift parcels of less than twenty kilograms.

If I had been thinking clearly, I would have immediately divided my goods into twenty-kilogram lots and sent them all through the post office. But, apart from the weight, the real problem was the oversized trunks that I had just purchased. I had found the trunks, purely by chance, at a secondhand furniture shop out near the old British South Park Street Cemetery. I had also been tempted by a wrought-iron four-poster bed with cast-iron finials and a soaring wirework mosquitonet support, but I managed to limit myself to the trunks. The sole purpose of my visit to that neighborhood of Calcutta was not to buy steamer trunks, but to look at the quirky British colonial gravestone inscriptions at the South Park Street Cemetery. The inscriptions gave tantalizing insights into several bizarre deaths. On one tombstone I discovered that the dearly departed was now resting in peace because of her addiction to mangoes. On another tombstone I learned that a man had been buried with his dog after some sort of hunting mishap.

The steamer trunks were from the days of the British Raj. Each one had stitched leather handles, riveted metal exteriors, and massive locks with working keys. The trunks were covered with evocative P&O shipping stamps, as well as hotel stickers from places like the Strand Hotel in Rangoon, the New Oriental Hotel in Galle (Sri Lanka), Raffles in Singapore, the Peninsula in Hong Kong, and my favorite, the Gymkhana Club in New Delhi. There was no obvious reason to send the trunks home empty and so I filled them to the brim with new purchases and the hodgepodge of treasures that I had been collecting over the previous year.

Once I had committed myself to the huge steamer trunks I had no other choice than to send them by sea through one of the numerous shipping companies that offer their services at the Calcutta Customs House. I set aside a week to complete the customs and shipping formalities, but after five days of strenuous effort it became obvious that I was going to be in Calcutta for quite some time. The hotel manager began to inquire about my proposed departure date and when I tried to sound reassuring by telling him I would be leaving in a matter of days he simply wobbled his head from side to side and said "*Acha*." The days slowly grew into weeks.

My first mistake was to try to organize all of the paperwork by myself. This was part of an intense, but short-lived, attempt to avoid paying a small commission to a shipping agent. To save the equivalent of $25 I spent my second week wandering through the debilitating heat of Calcutta. I made dozens of visits to the Customs House, the Reserve Bank of India, three different shipping companies, and an insurance agent before I got a feel for the huge scope of my undertaking. There were port charges to be calculated, shipping surcharges, cooperage fees, a bunker surcharge, as well as payment for documentation, typing, stamps, paper, and carbon paper. There was also the obvious problem of how to transport the trunks to the docks. No rickshaw could bear the weight, and I was uncertain how to arrange for a bullock cart or a small truck.

I applied for an export permit from the Deputy Controller at the Exchange Control Department at the Reserve Bank of India. The man was sympathetic, but he made it clear that I would first have to establish, in rupees, the value of each item. This was for insurance purposes. I returned to my hotel room where I unpacked the trunks and estimated, as best I could, the value of things such as a secondhand Robin Bannerjee movie poster and the dried bodies of the nine *Dorcus giraffa* beetles I had collected in the Khasi Hills of Assam. Another week passed, but each time progress began to seem like a possibility, a new set of permits, signatures and rubber-stamp impressions had to be collected, and paid for. The more I discovered about the shipping business in India, the less I understood how the process worked. Numerous complications and delays followed, but it wasn't until the pile of documents and permits grew to fifty-three pages that I felt the first cold sweat of panic.

On the recommendation of the hotel manager, I went to visit his second cousin, a Mr. J. B. Mukharjee at the Indian Mercantile Agency. As I approached the imposing stone facade of the Customs House I was slowly caught up by a chattering tide of office workers that surged into a huge hall where men, carrying trays of tea or with their arms full of bulging folders, crammed the aisles between the rows of desks piled high with yellowed forms. Antiquated telephones rang constantly and frantic shouts came from every direction. The impact of thousands of typewriter keys against paper, and the thunderous pounding of rubber stamps and staplers made normal conversation impossible.

Surrounded by this scene of chaos, Mr. Mukharjee sat at his desk looking remarkably composed. He was a heavyset man dressed in an immaculate white dhoti and a long shirt, the sleeves and tails of which rustled in the breeze of an overhead ceiling fan. Mr. Mukharjee's lips were stained a blood-red color from chewing pan and his catlike eyes were lined with kohl. Mr. Mukharjee shook my hand and gestured with a nod of his head to an empty chair. He ordered tea and then gave my pile of documents a cursory glance before chuckling to himself and setting them aside. He asked a few questions, then offered to handle all arrangements, including shipping charges, for 2,137 rupees (approximately $275 U.S.). I wasn't sure how he came to that precise amount so quickly, but it seemed reasonable and I agreed to the price. My only stipulation was that the wooden crate and the steamer trunks were, from that moment forth, to be the sole responsibility of J. B. Mukharjee and the Indian Mercantile Agency. He assured me that there would be no problems.

"My very, very dear friend, you have absolutely nothing to worry about!" said Mr. Mukharjee. He sat back in his chair and smiled at me with thick, fleshy, betel-nut-stained lips. Just the sight of him made me worry.

By the end of the week I was back at Mr. Mukharjee's desk filling out a thirty-six-page shipping manifest in triplicate because he had run out of carbon paper. I am not quite sure why I didn't go buy him a few new sheets of carbon paper, or why I felt compelled to try to speed up a process that I did not understand, but it wasn't long before I was once again spending my days collecting signatures and documents. The only noticeable difference in my routine was that I was now paying Mr. Mukharjee for the privilege of doing his work. I wandered around Calcutta from one warren of dimly lit office cubicles to the next and within days the heat and confusion drained me of all reason.

"Patience, my good friend, patience," Mr. Mukharjee implored.

The purpose of retaining a shipping agent who appeared to do very little didn't sink in until much later. But by then I was too distracted by the task of obtaining a Tax Clearance

Certificate from the Foreign Section of the Income Tax Department to give the matter much thought. I remained positive but confused and found myself spending most of my time waiting uncertainly. I was looking for a sign, for tangible proof, that progress was being made. The extent of Mr. Mukharjee's nonchalance remained unclear until the day he interrupted one of our conversations to eat lunch. On his desk he arranged my shipping documents like a place mat, then set out a stack of chappatis, a tin plate, and some bowls of rice and dal. The sight of him preparing his meal on top of those hard-earned documents had a sobering effect on me and I found myself wondering if, at the conclusion of his lunch, he would be using one of those precious forms as a table napkin.

"It is time for my tiffin," he said.

I excused myself and walked back to the hotel in a special state of calmness that was the result of intense feelings of frustration and anxiety. I stayed away from J. B. Mukharjee and the Indian Mercantile Agency for a few days and during that time I thought about how I might help facilitate the process. I drew on my years of experience in Asia to find a workable solution. According to Indian tradition there are four ways of achieving a goal, namely: *sama* (conciliation), *dana* (gifts or bribery), *bheda* (sowing dissension), or *panda* (the use of force). I figured the dana gambit was the most likely way to get results from J. B. Mukharjee, but no amount of flattery or my blatant offers of "gratuities" seemed to motivate him. J. B. Mukharjee was an enigma. His habit of quietly chuckling to himself in response to my comments had me dumbfounded. I just couldn't understand the man. He seemed mysterious and unknowable, but as the days went by,

and the first faint signs of progress appeared, I began to wonder if he was quietly working his vast web of contacts on my
behalf. The other possibility was that I had hired a betel-nut-
chewing nightmare to help me. In any event, I was at his
mercy and this seemed just fine with J. B. Mukharjee.

Then I met Jacqueline, a young Frenchwoman who lived
in my hotel. I didn't know it at the time, but she made it possible for me to move from a position of frustration and uncertainty to a state of acceptance and grace. The transformation
began with a simple suggestion. At breakfast one morning,
she told me she worked in the women's ward at a place called
Mother Teresa's Home for the Dying Destitute. Up until that
morning, I had never heard of Mother Teresa or her work.
Jacqueline described the home, commonly known as the
Kalighat Clinic, as a place for poor homeless people to die in
peace. The alternative, as I had witnessed on several occasions, was to die in public; out on the streets where these
people were unprotected from the sun and rain and where
they were sometimes preyed upon by scavenging dogs, rats
and carrion birds. As I sat at our breakfast table sipping tea
and thinking about what it would be like to die on the streets
of Calcutta, Jacqueline invited me to visit Mother Teresa's
Home for the Dying Destitute. Without giving it much
thought, I wrote down her directions on how to find the place.

The following morning at dawn, I climbed aboard the
crowded Kalighat tram as it rumbled and lurched and
screeched its way south, along Chowringhee Street. Sparks
crackled from the overhead power lines and the smell of
burning brakes, jasmine blossoms and coconut-scented hair

oil mingled in the warm morning air. I stepped off the tram near the Kali temple and walked for five minutes along a labyrinth of laneways that were quite unfamiliar to me. Through a break in the traffic I caught sight of a typical Calcutta scene. At roadside, inches from the ebb and flow of trucks, bicyclists, pedestrians, rickshaws and wandering cows, a photograph was being taken of a dead man on a slightly inclined bed surrounded by his family. Several garlands of marigolds hung around his neck. The photographer's head was obscured by the black cloth draped over a large-format camera perched on a wooden tripod with thin, varnished legs and polished brass fittings. The dead man was wearing a pair of round tortoiseshell spectacles and his hair had been freshly pomaded and combed for a final family portrait. When the photographer finished his work the bed was lifted high by the men and carried in the direction of the nearby burning ghats for public cremation at the edge of the Hooghly River.

I became lost and so I stopped to ask for directions from a fortune teller who was sitting in the shade of an overturned Nash Ambassador car leaning against a tree. Judging from the rust and accumulated road dirt, it looked like it had been there for decades. The man pointed me in the right direction and I continued walking until I came upon a goat being held by two men. One man steadied the hind legs while the other man pulled the body taut with a short piece of cord looped around the horns. A third man stepped forward and hacked off the animal's head with a single stroke from a heavy cleaver. The head flopped on the ground and a moment later a torrent of blood gushed from the neck and onto the rough cobbles. But I had already witnessed the decapitation of a full-grown water buffalo on the streets of Kathmandu months earlier, so I didn't stay to watch.

A few moments later I found what I was looking for: a sign perched over a doorway that read: Nirmal Hriday—Home for Dying Destitutes. Reading the sign, the first thought that came to mind were the words "Normal Holiday." It was only much later that I learned "Nirmal Hriday" means "the place of the pure heart." I entered the building and introduced myself to Sister Luke. She welcomed me, and after I explained that I would like to work as a volunteer for the day she assigned one of the Sisters to give me a brief tour of the building. As we walked between the rows of low cots, I couldn't help but think to myself: "This is definitely not a normal holiday . . . and what am I doing here?"

A soft light filtered through a bank of high windows illuminating a haunting scene where about sixty men lay in rows on stretchers. Some of the people were being fed intravenously, while others had tubes in their noses. Brothers tapped at forearms searching for veins, and the antiseptic smell of Dettol partially masked the odor of the sick and dying. The quiet atmosphere and austere look of the place somehow lent dignity to the stark scenes of people at the end of their lives. On the far side of a central courtyard the women were taken care of in a similar ward. I came with the expectation of being repulsed by horrifying scenes and foul smells, but despite the sad sight of so many helpless, tired and emaciated bodies the building was remarkably clean and well ordered. It was clear that many of these people would last only a few days, but there was no sense of panic or terror, and from the first moment I entered the building I was filled with an unexpected feeling of peace and tranquillity. I was prepared to be shocked by the worst Calcutta had to offer, but instead, I simply followed my instructions and got down to doing what needed to be done—ministering to the dying poor of Calcutta, a job that I was completely unprepared for.

The job was straightforward enough. I bathed, fed and comforted the inhabitants of the men's ward. That first morning I found myself doing things I had never imagined doing. A beautiful young Anglo-Indian Sister, in her coarsely woven white sari with a border of indigo-blue stripes, showed me how to clean festering sores with forceps, cotton wool and a shallow pan full of potassium permanganate and water. A man with empty eye sockets lay motionless on his cot as we cleaned a wound on his hip that was alive with maggots. He must have been in pain, but he never flinched. The fixed smile on his face made me wonder if he was dead and if the smile was merely a grimace fixed in place by rigor mortis. But I could see his chest rise and fall slightly with each shallow breath. He was still holding onto life. We dressed his wounds and moved to the next person without speaking. I found myself watching the Sister's delicate hands at work. They were gentle but also purposeful and experienced. Her posture and every motion conveyed a sense of loving-kindness and a luminosity of spirit.

There was little to say in such a place. Devastated by old age, malnutrition and illness, many of the patients, with their battered, worn-out bodies, must have been suffering terribly, but they rested quietly without complaint as we worked on them. I shifted from the side of one cot to the next in a trance, sometimes watching the Sister work and sometimes helping. One old man spat up a great wad of bloody phlegm which we washed away. His condition continued to deteriorate throughout the morning. By noon he was dead. His body was carried away and within an hour another man, in an equally feeble state, was placed on the cot that still bore the impression of its previous occupant. Looking around the ward, I took in the scene and in doing so I couldn't be sure if I was witnessing something horrible, or something beautiful. Whatever it was, I found myself transported by the intensity and clarity of purpose that permeated the place.

I carried emaciated men to the courtyard where I sat them on plastic sheets and washed them with buckets of lukewarm water and soap. I propped them upright with one knee placed behind their backs so they wouldn't topple over and toweled them dry before dressing them in sarongs and carrying them back to their cots. I sprinkled their bodies with talcum powder where bedsores were beginning to form, and shifted men from one cot to another. The bodies were practically weightless. I fed men with a spoon and poured water down their throats from a measuring cup. One man's body was so wasted away that when I rubbed powder on his chest my fingers vibrated over the deep furrows between his ribs. I was mesmerized by the people's courage and their dignified attitude toward pain and death. This made me think about acceptance without resignation, and it goes without saying that by mid-morning of my first day at the Kalighat Clinic, I had forgotten about J. B. Mukharjee.

In Mother Teresa's Home for the Dying Destitute there

was a complete lack of panic and desperation. It was a place where human life was completely unveiled, stripped bare; where one could watch, take part in, and accept the inevitability of death with grace. What I witnessed that first day was not something terrible or repulsive, but rather noble and uplifting, and I think that this sensation contributed to my decision to return the following morning.

On my second day a boy by the name of Aman Datta indicated that he wanted me to shave his head because of the stifling heat. I cut his thick, black curls down to a stubble with a pair of surgical scissors, then scrubbed away a thick layer of road grime and dead skin to get to the scalp. I lathered his head and started to shave him with an old-fashioned double-bladed safety razor—the kind that look like they are designed not to cut into the flesh any deeper than a quarter of an inch. I worked slowly and as I negotiated the irregular terrain of lumps and old scars, I was careful not to cut him. I wondered about the history of each scar. It looked like he had been clubbed over the head at some point in his short life. The haircut transformed his sweet-looking face, and by the time I finished his sunken eyes and shining pate made him look delicate and fragile. Without his luxurious head of hair he lost his individuality and blended in with the other men around him.

Aman was dying from tuberculosis. He was so thin that when the Brothers came to give him an injection they had a difficult time finding a spot on his body with enough muscle. The large needle didn't pierce the skin on his hip, so they used a small magnifying glass to inspect the point. Since it appeared sharp they simply used more force the second time until the needle penetrated the skin. I remember thinking to myself, "He is too young to die." A week later I carried his lifeless body to the morgue.

I became one of the regular volunteers. Some days I would ride the Kalighat tram with Jacqueline, but more often than not I arrived by myself at around six A.M. and then worked until about midday, four or five days each week. Afternoons were often spent with Mr. Mukharjee, who gradually began to reveal his mastery of import/export protocol and documentation. Surely, India must have one of the world's most cumbersome bureaucracies, but J. B. Mukharjee began to deftly solve each and every problem that arose. He took delight in introducing me to the fine points of his profession. For Mr. Mukharjee it was all a wonderful voyage of discovery, a puzzle to be solved—a game of wits to be played like cricket. It was all about strategy, testing of limits (including mine), and finessing his way through the growing paper storm that left me stupefied, but which made his heart pound and his spirit soar. Or so I imagined.

The work at Mother Teresa's had an unexpected and soothing effect on me. I grew to appreciate the futility of my previous efforts to deal with my steamer trunks. This helped to lessen the dread that gripped me every time I entered the Customs House. Looking back, it seems odd that the Home of the Dying Destitute had such a calming effect because, day after day, I was drawn into situations that were far from comforting. Things like dealing with a human arm gnawed to the bone by sewer rats or seeing part of an old man's face chewed away by street dogs. Scenes not easily forgotten, even now, after the passage of twenty-seven years. Half a lifetime.

During my time at Mother Teresa's I seldom gave a thought to what might happen to my own health if I caught some infectious disease. At the end of each day I washed my hands and forearms in a bucket of Dettol and water. Apart from this basic precaution, I simply reassured myself that, in exchange for my work, I was protected by divine guidance.

Every week or so curious Westerners dropped by the Kalighat Clinic for a quick look. The few of them who had the gall to take photographs immediately disappeared as if they had captured something of great value. One morning an elderly Japanese man arrived with a collapsible easel and a small wooden case. He bowed deeply to the Sisters and introduced himself as Mr. Yuki Suzuki. After a brief conversation, the man spent the morning quietly moving around the ward looking at the men and studying the play of light and shadow on their bodies. He taped a piece of paper on his drawing board and began making pencil sketches. It seemed macabre, and I expected his work to look something like the voyeuristic photography of cripples, corpses and body-part still life studies by Joel-Peter Witkin. But looking at Mr. Suzuki's work I realized that, for him, the ward, filled with prostrate bodies, skin-covered bones and wasted limbs, presented haunting abstract shapes and patterns. The drawings were beautifully rendered. They also conveyed great compassion and respect. Prior arrangements must have been made with the Sisters, but I was mildly shocked to see him at work surrounded by all of the expected activities and sights and sounds associated with the dying destitute of Calcutta.

Watching Mr. Suzuki at work, it occurred to me that any activity at the clinic seemed permissible and appropriate as long as it was done with thoughtfulness and sincerity. Had Mr. Suzuki been less sensitive or less skilled I doubt the Sisters would have allowed him to stay. I had never thought of protruding rib cages and hip bones as being something beautiful, but his pencil sketches, and later the watercolors, made me think about what I was doing in the men's ward. I had no justification to feel self-righteous because it was clear to me that his motivations were more pure than mine. He was documenting, in a very personal way, the simple truth of Mother Teresa's work—the sacred and unconditional love of human life. I was partially drawn to the Kalighat Clinic in hopes of quieting my mind while dealing with J. P. Mukharjee, but I also knew that a part of me craved exposure to what I thought would be the worst scenes of human degradation that India had to offer. It didn't thrill me to witness and participate in these discomforting scenes, but I wanted to experience illness and death up close—immediate, personal and real. There was nothing abstract about helping people die.

By the time Mr. Suzuki arrived, I had somehow convinced myself that my work at Mother Teresa's might be a way of giving something back to humanity for all of the insights into human nature, and, by extension, my own nature, that I had gained from living in Asia for nearly four years. But of course it was sheer naïveté that made me think I was the one who was doing the giving at Mother Teresa's. Partially through Mr. Suzuki's work, I came to the realization that once again I was receiving life lessons, only this time they came from dying strangers.

Practically every day phrases came to me while I worked. I repeated and meditated silently on thoughts such as: "Know suffering." . . . "Death with dignity." . . . "Give hope to the hopeless." . . . "We are enriched by our random acts of love and kindness." . . . "Know the truth through compassion."

Who knows where these messages came from? They were not voices I heard, but rather phrases clearly written in my mind's eye. This had never happened to me before. I found it all very strange, but I focused on these messages and repeated them to myself while I worked. One basic issue continued to occupy my mind. I knew that the Sisters and Brothers were doing this work for the love of God, but as the weeks went by I couldn't help but ask myself the obvious questions about why I was doing the work, and for whom, and what higher purpose I was serving, if any. Despite not being able to clarify why I was working at Mother Teresa's, I simply continued to show up every day because it felt right. "Fulfillment of being" is about as close as I have ever come to providing an explanation for why I continued to work at the clinic, and perhaps I should just leave it at that.

But there were lighter moments as well, and as anyone who has worked for Mother Teresa will tell you, laughter and humor is an essential component of compassion and love. I befriended a half-wit orderly by the name of Mark Anthony. He slept in the ward alongside the dead and dying. The morning I met him he was wandering around the toilets trying to swat flies out of the air with an old broom handle.

"Flies I am killing!" he exclaimed with a shrill laugh.

Anthony (as he preferred to be called) spoke broken English, but he was fluent in Hindi, Malayalam, Bengali, and Tamil. He was an unlikely linguist, but the Sisters and Brothers welcomed his presence because he was useful as a translator. One day Anthony asked if he could borrow my razor. I slipped a new blade into the razor and handed it to him. Then Anthony disappeared onto the rooftop with a bar of soap and a pan of water. When he reappeared twenty minutes later his face was bleeding freely from a mass of superficial cuts. My first thought was that he had opened the razor and shaved himself with the bare blade.

"Have I missed anything?" he asked.

"Yes, I believe you missed your nose and your throat," I joked.

"The blood? Oh, yes . . . there has been some cutting I think!" The razor and his hand were covered in blood as he stood there laughing hysterically.

A man who was too weak to sit up in his cot gestured to me that he needed to urinate. I brought him the pee bottle and as I lifted his sarong I caught sight of his penis. I was shocked at the size of it. For such a frail old man it seemed impossibly long and thick. The girth was impressive. I thought it possible that it was the contrast with his emaciated body that made his penis seem so big, but I wasn't sure, until the man began to chuckle. Looking at him, I realized he must have read my thoughts. He definitely had a whopper and even in his feeble state it was abundantly clear that one part of his anatomy still appeared to be in perfectly good working order.

I continued to give the men haircuts and shaves and by the end of the second week I started trimming fingernails and toenails. One man had an index finger that sprouted two identical tips from the first joint. Each tip had its own corrugated fingernail, and I took my time to do a good job. When I was finished with the scissors I cleaned beneath his nails and pushed down the cuticles before continuing with the nail file. It was unnecessary to do such a meticulous job, but when I was finished I held his hand away from me as if I were carefully scrutinizing the work for any minor imperfections. He watched me add a few deft strokes before he raised his eyebrows and nodded his approval. Then we both broke out in laughter.

Two days later the man with the double fingertip motioned for me to sit by his cot. I stroked the center of his chest for a while and he seemed to like that. He was too weak to talk, but in any event we had no language in common. That morning his breathing seemed shallow . . . What I remember most about the man were his eyelashes; he had the longest eyelashes I have ever seen. I sat next to him and held his hand for a few minutes before turning to take care of the man in the next cot. By the time I looked back, the man with the long eyelashes had relaxed his grip and he was motionless. I touched his forearm and it felt different. There was no pulse at his neck, his eyes were wide open and he had stopped breathing. For a few moments I sat there without moving, wondering what was wrong. I had seen dead people before, but this was the first time in my life that someone had died right beside me. It seemed impossible that life could go out of a body with such ease. In the space of a minute he passed from living to being dead without a sound. In a lifetime, how many opportunities would I have to hold a stranger's hand and keep him company as he died? Stunned by the experience, I took a deep breath and sat speechless by the cot for a while before notifying one of the Sisters. She placed a stethoscope to his chest, listened, and then confirmed that he was dead. She closed his eyelids and I carried the man to the cool room in the courtyard, where I placed him on a concrete slab. Before returning to the men's ward, I took one last look at his long eyelashes, and his perfectly trimmed fingernails. All eleven of them. At the end of the day a Hindu organization took the body, along with others, to the burning ghats for cremation.

Two months passed. By then the hotel manager had reluctantly agreed to a weekly rate for my room, but I was getting no closer to shipping my things to San Francisco. The freight costs and shipping dates seemed to be recalculated according to the weather, but by this time J. B. Mukharjee was firmly in control. We politely discussed petty extra charges on a daily basis, deciding which ones to ignore and which ones to refuse to pay. One miserably hot afternoon the shipping documents and permits were finally assembled into a pile that was more than an inch thick. Thinking this was the end of my ordeal, I offered to take the crate and trunks to the Kidderpore Docks where a freighter was due to leave for the West Coast of the United States. Mr. Mukharjee advised against this plan, and explained that for a small additional fee he would complete the job.

"Please . . . There might be some complications for you," he cautioned me.

"Complications? But what could possibly go wrong at this point?" I said.

"What could go wrong?" He laughed. "Oh, my friend, my very dear friend, many things could go wrong. Unimaginable things." J. B. Mukharjee chuckled as he placed another wad of pan in his mouth. He seemed lost in thought as he considered the delectable possibilities.

Pilferage between my hotel and the docks seemed a

remote possibility, but it must have been the imaginary threat of theft that encouraged me to accompany the trunks and crate to the docks and onboard the ship. When Mr. Mukharjee sensed I was determined to handle the transportation he merely gestured with a shrug of his shoulders and upturned palms and advised me to do as I pleased.

The following day, accompanied by frightful explosions from the tailpipe of a lurching and battered three-wheeled truck, I arrived at the Kidderpore Docks in a dense cloud of exhaust fumes and scorching hot dust. Unfortunately, no one had told me that I would need a permit to pass through the main gate. The barefoot truck driver took me a short distance to the Office of Permits where I met with the Superintendent of Permits. The man took so long issuing me a one-day pass that by the time we returned to the gate the docks were closed to deliveries for the rest of the day. The port would be shut for the next two days, for unknown reasons, and this meant that the ship would sail before I could return. When I realized that I would now have to transport the trunks and crate back to the hotel, then find another ship, hire another truck to come back to the dock, and apply for another gate pass, my mind suddenly went numb. I stared dumbly at the closed gate, the gate-keeper holding my recently expired gate pass, my feet, the ground at my feet, the cracks in the pavement, the dead grass and particles of sand in the cracks. Emerging from a crack in the pavement, an ant struggled beneath the weight of a huge seed. Realizing the ant was going back to its nest, it occurred to me that at least one of us had a clear purpose to justify our efforts.

Then, without warning, I started to laugh. I laughed until

the tears streamed down my cheeks. I laughed until I couldn't speak, and the driver, unable to restrain himself, joined in. We sat at the side of the road laughing as we inhaled the fumes of the oil-drenched earth baking in the mid-afternoon sun. When we finally regained our composure, my first instinct was to leave the trunks and the crate at the side of the road and be done with them. But instead, the driver turned the truck around and, like the ant, we headed back to the nest—the teeming, sweltering center of Calcutta.

In the debilitating heat of late afternoon I returned to my hotel in a state of collapse. The crate and trunks were lugged through the front gate and stacked in the courtyard. I could see the manager's face framed by a window on the second floor. He surveyed the commotion, pursed his lips at the sight of my return, tapped his fingertips together as if in prayer, lifted his eyebrows and then turned slowly on his heel and disappeared from sight. The sweepers in the courtyard were too polite to comment. Instead, they wobbled their heads from side to side and busied themselves by working their brooms over the already immaculate courtyard.

I may have developed a greater appreciation for the transforming power of patience through my work at the Home for the Dying Destitute, but that day at the Kidderpore Docks was a watershed experience. False hope and illusion fell away and I surrendered myself, my steamer trunks and the packing crate to Mr. Mukharjee, and to fate. I made it clear that I would no longer meddle with his work. J. P. Mukharjee chuckled to himself, briefly, as if enjoying a private joke, and then ordered tea. A week later the trunks and crate were picked up from the hotel, sent out to the docks, and hoisted aboard the freighter *Vishva Prayas*. It was a small feat, but it was as if Mr. Mukharjee had performed a miracle. I had been in Calcutta nearly three months, and now it was with mixed emotions that I watched the rusted freighter slip its moorings and move down the Hooghly River on the outgoing tide. Would I ever see my belongings again? I asked myself. At that point it no longer seemed to matter.

Several days later, when I was ready to leave Mother Teresa's, I thanked Sister Luke and told her what a privilege it had been to work at the clinic. I located Anthony, who was busy trying to kill flies by snapping them against the wall with a large rubber band. I handed him a new razor, a packet of blades and an envelope full of Band-Aids and he laughed. He said good-bye in each of his many languages and then I walked out the door for the last time. With a few short steps I moved from the relative peace and quiet of Mother Teresa's Home for the Dying Destitute back into the seething chaos on the streets of Calcutta. Jostled and bumped by the crush of bodies, and deafened by a cacophony of honking horns and human voices, I took in the sights and sounds and smells of the city. Without hesitation or doubt, I joined this sea of humanity with a calmness, clarity of purpose, and a lightness of being that have never left me.

Cooking with Madame Zoya

THE FIRST AFTERNOON I went to call on Madame Zoya, I had only a vague idea of where I was going. I set off thinking the journey to her apartment in the Washington Heights neighborhood of Manhattan was going to be a simple matter of picking up several platters of Russian food from her for a friend's birthday party. But the further I drove uptown, the more uneasy I became. I arrived at the front of a badly deteriorated apartment building on a dead-end street strewn with garbage. I was certain I had written down the wrong address, but when I checked the street and number I realized, with a sinking feeling in my stomach, that I had the right place. Young men wielding baseball bats leaned against battered cars and a chain-link fence. I stepped out of my car but before I could lock the door behind me, a man was at my side offering drugs and sex. I told him I wasn't interested. He looked me in the eye and said real slow, "You need someone protect yo' car." It wasn't a question.

There was no intercom or security system at the front of Madame Zoya's building and when I opened the front door, I stopped short because an unchained pit bull was standing at the side of the small lobby. The dog bared his teeth, then lifted his leg and pissed on the tile wall. A man was squatting on the lobby floor eating spaghetti and meatballs with his fingers off a piece of crumpled aluminum foil. He took a brief look at me and then shouted "SPOOKY!" and the animal backed off.

The doorman on his lunch break, I thought to myself.

The corridors were strewn with empty bottles and the building smelled of rotting garbage and cigarette butts. I didn't have the nerve to take the elevator because of the possibility of being trapped there by someone with a baseball bat and a need for the contents of my pockets, which unfortunately contained $600 in cash for Madame Zoya. I climbed a darkened stairway, but before I reached the second floor I stuffed the money into my right sock. On the fourth floor, at the end of a deserted hallway, I knocked on a door. I identified myself, then heard the distinctive thud and clank and rattle of locks and security chains being manipulated. The door opened.

"You hat no trouble finding me?" Madame Zoya said.

Madame Zoya appeared to be in her mid-eighties. Her hair had turned white, yet she had the complexion and demeanor of a woman thirty years younger. Her sly flirtatious laugh and deep-green Slavic eyes attracted me at once and provided a clue as to what a beauty she must have been in her youth.

I walked through the door and entered a time warp. With a single step I moved from the mean streets and crack cocaine dealers of Washington Heights to the cozy comfort of an apartment in St. Petersburg in 1930. All the book titles were in

Russian. Framed and signed watercolor paintings of Russian fairy tales and photos of Czar Nicholay II and Czarina Aleksandra hung from the walls. There were deep red Persian carpets on the perfectly maintained oak floors. The sight of mahogany tables, an old samovar and the smell of carnauba paste wax transported me to a different time and place. Arranged on a side table was a collection of nesting wooden dolls and hand-painted lacquer boxes illustrating scenes from the stories of Alexander Pushkin. On a shelf, flanked by Russian medical texts, I noticed a black-and-white photograph of Rudolph Nureyev as a very young man. The photo was inscribed to Madame Zoya.

Through a gap in the lace curtains I caught a narrow glimpse of the neighborhood. The space between two buildings was piled high with discarded refrigerators, broken toys, auto parts, garbage, rotting mattresses, takeaway food containers and bashed-in television sets. An urban midden pile, with a complicated story to tell to some future urban archaeologist.

I felt safe inside the apartment, but during that first visit I only stayed long enough to pick up the food and pay Madame Zoya. She would arrive by cab at my apartment to help serve the meal that night, but I had offered to drive her home after the dinner.

I remember very little of that evening, which was a seventieth birthday party for Philippe Braunschweig, the creator of the Prix de Lausanne international ballet competition and a patron of the choreographer Maurice Béjart. Jock Soto and Wendy Whelan plus several dancers from the corps de ballet from the New York City Ballet showed up along with the dance critic Anna Kisselgoff from the *New York Times*. There were Knight Landesmann from *Art Forum*; the graffiti artist Futura 2000 and his wife, Ceci; Keith Sonnier and his Brazilian wife, Nessia; Harvey Lichtenstein, then the director of the Brooklyn Academy of Music; the art dealer and gallery owner Holly Solomon; the artist Donald Baechler; and Michael Avedon, Richard's brother. The room pulsated with energy.

Most of the conversation that evening revolved around ballet, especially the French star Sylvie Guillem and her work with the choreographer William Forsythe of the Frankfurt Ballet. People discussed a recent performance of Laurie Anderson, the upcoming Warhol auction, and likely possibilities for fund-raising. After years of promising, Christophe de Menil finally remembered to give me her mother's family recipe for steamed Christmas pudding, but a good deal of my time was spent in nervous anticipation of driving Madame Zoya home. I wondered what her neighborhood would be like after dark. At about eleven P.M. I found out.

I eased the car to a stop at the corner of Broadway and West 139th Street. Madame Zoya placed her hand on my forearm and thanked me for the ride. When I told her I would take her to the door she let out a flirtatious giggle and said, "Well, you are very sweet and kind man and I thank you for the offer, but I think not tonight." Then, in a more serious voice she said, "I am safe here, but at this hour you are not. Lock your doors and drive away. Good night to you. Go now." I watched her as she walked down the unlit street. The glowing red tips of cigarettes flared. Dark forms moved in the shadows.

Nearly six months went by before I found the nerve to pay Madame Zoya a second visit. I had promised myself not to go back to the neighborhood, but when she invited me to come see how she prepared pickled herring and pelmeni, I accepted. Where else would I ever learn the proper way to make these dishes? She recited a shopping list to me over the phone and three days later I was back in the lobby of her building with bags of groceries from Zabar's and Fairway Market. On my way to the stairs at the far end of her lobby, I passed by a series of identical pockmarks in the shattered tile wall. Running my fingers over the jagged depressions I couldn't help but think they looked like bullet holes. When I asked Madame Zoya about the pockmarks in the lobby, she told me the story.

"Vat kind of animal world do we live in these days?" she said. "I was havink a dinner party. I hear a knock on the door and it is my friend George. He is late and there are these two strange men standing behind him. I don't know these men.

"'And who have you brought with you, George?'" I asked him.

"'Zoya, it is not I who have brought these men . . . it is they who have brought me.'"

One of the men stepped forward and showed his FBI badge. "May we come in?" he asked. "But of course," said Madame Zoya.

There had been a shoot-out in the lobby and a corpse lay sprawled on the marble floor. Blood and gore, bone fragments and brain tissue, spent bullet casings and drug vials were scattered everywhere, and the front entrance to the building was temporarily closed. George was led to Madame Zoya's apartment by way of the basement and a set of back stairs. George described how he followed the men through a mildewed warren of darkened passageways where leaking steam pipes hissed and a damp chill emanated from the floors and walls. Water dripped and the scurrying sounds of sewer rats came from somewhere in the jumbles of broken furniture, just visible in the yellow beam of the flashlights.

"Now, what can you tell us about the gunshots?" the agent asked Madame Zoya.

"Which ones do you mean?" she said. "If I pay attention to every gunshot and scream in this neighborhood I vill never have time to do anything else. Some days I am working on preparing my food and there is the gunshots, I say to myself *Boje moy!* [My God!], how can I get these piroshki done in time for the party with all this commotion? What can I do? I can do nothing, so I turn up the music on the radio and then I can concentrate again."

There was a pause as she suddenly remembered her other guests. "Oh, my God!" Madame Zoya exclaimed. "There are two older ladies, teachers from School of American Ballet, comeink to dinner and they are expected now. What am I to do? If they see the det body they will never come to dinner again." The FBI agents offered to go down to the street and escort the ladies to Madame Zoya's apartment. But first the agents wanted to know what the women looked like. "Do not you worry." Madame Zoya laughed. "In dis neighborhood you cannot miss them I think."

The agents went back downstairs and a short while later they led two women through the basement maze and up the back stairs to the apartment. The women wore fur coats and they carried bottles of champagne and a bouquet of flowers. They were delighted that the two handsome men had taken them on *la petite aventure*. Excusing themselves, the FBI agents returned to their work. After the body had been bagged and removed, and statements and names had been taken, the two men returned to Madame Zoya's door.

"Yes?" Madame Zoya said.

"Please excuse us, but what is this marvelous smell coming from your apartment?"

"Oh, this is just some Russian cooking."

"Do you think we could try just a bite?"

"And vie not? There are three ladies and only one gentleman. Please, come in!"

The meal was accompanied by the champagne and then the glasses of frozen vodka came out. The FBI agents rolled back the carpets and the dancing began. One of the women took off her high heels and danced in her stockings on the dining-room floor. She performed a series of pirouettes, followed by a *développé* and a *soutenus,* before finishing with a graceful port de bras. Much later, and with far less skill, the FBI agents danced with Madame Zoya and the other women to Russian gypsy music.

"So you see. In spite of the det body, we had a good time," Madame Zoya told me. "But never mind that. Now I have some hairink for you. So please, you will also have some vodka.

"Nasdarovia!" said Madame Zoya, raising her glass.

"Nasdarovia, " I said.

We placed the empty shot glasses on the table and refilled them. It was approximately 10:30 on a Wednesday morning.

"Now, for your energy, you must hev, each day, two pieces prepared salted hairink. First some butter on the black bread like dis, then the hairink . . . and some slice-ed onion. This I know for the fact: hairink will give you energy. Make you strong. I cannot live without the hairink, and once you try, you will see that you cannot live without the hairink." I tried the herring. It was delicious, flavorful and well prepared, the best I have ever had—but even then I knew in my heart that I could live without it.

Madame Zoya worked out of a small kitchen in her apartment where she used a four-burner stove with a standard size oven and refrigerator. To save space in the refrigerator during the winter months, she kept fresh herring and other perishable food outside on the wide and deeply inset kitchen windowsill of her fourth-floor apartment. From this tiny kitchen she once prepared a buffet dinner for more than one thousand people. When I met Madame Zoya she preferred to keep the numbers down to 150 people or less. Even for a party of 150 people this meant preparing five hundred piroshki, three hundred blini, and ten pounds of eggplant caviar. She worked off an eight-inch by ten-inch wooden cutting board on a three-foot-wide kitchen table. Madame Zoya did her own shopping by bus and frequently delivered the food by cab. Business had tapered off in recent years, but she lived in a rent-controlled apartment and this helped her get by on a couple of dinners or cocktail party receptions each month. I never heard her complain once. She lived simply and was grateful that she had never been forced to sell her jewelry or furniture. It was during my monthly visits over the following year that I managed to slowly piece together her story.

Madame Zoya was born in Simbirsk, Lenin's birthplace. She spent the early years of her childhood at "Prince Mountain," the family country house where there was a large staff to tend to her and her eight brothers and sisters. But then the Bolsheviks came and the family fled to the Crimea hoping to find a boat to Istanbul. They arrived too late, the port was closed and they were forced to return to Moscow. "That," Madame Zoya said, "was the beginning of the nightmare life. We were so poor. Poor just like the mouse in the church." For the next seven years the family lived in terrible poverty. When her grandmother died the body lay in the house for six days because there was no money for the burial. Not knowing what else to do, Madame Zoya's father went to the dentist, where he had a gold bridge removed. A jeweler gave him ninety rubles for the gold and with that money the grandmother was buried.

"Prince Mountain" was stripped of all family furniture and other items and turned into a state museum, but there were no exhibits or visitors. Madame Zoya grew up to become a nurse in an army hospital in Moscow during World War II. She spent her days taking care of the soldiers and dreaming about sitting in her mother's kitchen watching the two elderly cooks as they prepared the food of her childhood. She longed to leave Russia, and during the German siege of Moscow Madame Zoya got her wish. The hospital was surrounded and captured by German soldiers. She spent the next three years in a prisoner-of-war camp near Munich. I asked how she survived the camp.

"I was young woman, and pretty. So of course there was a way for me. A German officer took care of me and was kind. I stayed alive, and that was the important thing I learn. To stay in this life, whatever it brings."

After the war she milked cows on a farm in Belgium, saved her money and eventually found her way to the United

States, where she married a civil engineer. They moved into the apartment where she still lives. The building is located on West 139th Street, not far from the Abyssinian Baptist Church. When she settled in the United States in 1958 Madame Zoya felt as if she had come to the land of dreams. At that time the neighborhood was the home to Russian émigrés and princes in exile. People kept flowers in window boxes and there were big parties to celebrate Easter as well as Russian Christmas on January 7th.

By the 1970s the character of the neighborhood began to change. Madame Zoya urged her husband to move from their apartment when the owner of the building told her that he would have to sell because the city was letting the area deteriorate. But they never moved, and when her husband died Madame Zoya was trapped. She was lonely and confused and didn't have a clear idea of what she should do with her life. Eventually she took a job as a nurse at the Columbia Presbyterian Hospital. One day a friend called to let her know that an aging Russian princess needed a nurse to take care of her at home. Madame Zoya went to talk with the woman.

"Blini . . . for sixty years I have dreamed of real Russian blini. Ahhh, what I would give for just one!" the princess said to Madame Zoya at their first meeting. Remembering the food from her mother's kitchen where the cooks had shown her how to prepare such things, Madame Zoya offered to make the blini. "What are you saying?" the princess exclaimed. "You are a nurse. What do you know about blini?"

"I will show you," said Madame Zoya.

The next day Madame Zoya brought her blini pans and the ingredients to the woman's kitchen. She prepared the blini and served them with melted butter, sour cream, caviar and a light sprinkling of fresh chives. The woman took a bite, paused for a long moment to savor the taste, and then said, "Zoya . . . you are hired."

Madame Zoya was hired by the princess as a nurse, but her first assignment was to prepare a dinner party for sixteen Russian aristocrats. At the conclusion of the evening the guests asked for Madame Zoya's telephone number, and within a few months she had left her job with the princess to devote herself to cooking and catering full-time. Within a year she was delivering food to midtown Russian restaurants whose cooks did not have the time or the training or skill to duplicate her creations.

For twenty-six years she catered the annual Christmas party for the New York City Ballet. In 1988, to help celebrate the fortieth anniversary of the company, she prepared five thousand piroshki in her apartment kitchen and her hands ached for days afterward. At one of the earlier parties, before his death in 1983, George Balanchine had taken Madame Zoya aside and told her, "Zoya, I am an artist of the ballet, and you are an artist of the kitchen." There were other big events to cater. One at the Metropolitan Museum for Prince Charles, and a reception for Igor and Vera Stravinsky. The staff at the Japanese Embassy in Washington, D.C., was addicted to her piroshki with cabbage. For those who knew traditional Russian home cooking, Madame Zoya was simply the best. Grace Kelly loved her food so much that she tried to persuade Madame Zoya to work for her in Monaco. Madame Zoya explained that she could not accept the offer because of her age, but also because her home was in America.

All of Madame Zoya's food was made by hand, the old way, with only the best ingredients. Her yeasted blini were not quite traditional because she used 75 percent white flour with 25 percent buckwheat flour. This lightened the pancake-like blini and made it more like a crepe without sacrificing the unique tangy taste, color and texture of heavier buckwheat blini. In addition to blini and piroshki, her specialties were coulibiac (salmon baked with dill, chopped hard-boiled eggs, parsley and kasha in a flaky pastry dough), kotletki and bitotehki (chicken and meat cutlets), baklazhannia ikra (puree of eggplant), and vareniki and pelmeni (two types of Russian ravioli). Her pelmeni were sublime. She formed them into ear-shaped ravioli, then stuffed them with a mixture of young lamb, beef, garlic, onion and parsley. Madame Zoya served pelmeni three ways: with a clear broth, with homemade sour cream, or in the way I prefer to serve them now myself— dipped in a mixture of melted butter, fresh lemon juice and a hint of Dijon mustard.

Madame Zoya taught me how to make paskha, which is a type of moist cheesecake with fruit, eggs and vanilla. More like a pudding than a cake, paskha is traditionally prepared during the Easter season. Madame Zoya told me where to buy a set of blini pans and then showed me the proper way to season and use them. We mixed the lightly yeasted buckwheat batter, let it sit, and then cooked the thin blini and ate them in various ways: with homemade sour cream and herring, with plenty of melted sweet cream butter. Sometimes we substituted smoked or salted fish or chopped egg and dill. Between bites, we sipped frozen vodka.

One day, between shot glasses of vodka and morsels of

pickled herring, Madame Zoya told me the story of how she had almost lost her leg in an automobile accident five years earlier. She was convinced the injury was only a fracture, but the doctor insisted on screwing a steel rod to her ankle bone. After she had paid more than $7,000 in fees, gangrene developed and the doctor gave her the news that he must cut off her leg. Madame Zoya told him: "God gave me my leg and God may take my leg, but not you!" After the gangrene crisis passed, the doctor tried to convince her to have plastic surgery to hide the terrible scar. "Plastic surgery?" Madame Zoya said. "Are you mad? I am not having beauty pageant at my age, and so let us not hear any more about plastic surgery."

Fearing for her health, Madame Zoya discharged herself from the hospital. It took her nine months to recover from the shoddy medical treatment. She cured herself by following instructions from a 120-year-old Russian book on herbal medicine that she had found at a *marché aux puces* in Paris in 1955. In addition to other remedies, she used powdered birch bark (prepared in her manual coffee grinder) to heal the scar on her ankle. Each day she took five to fifteen drops of Saint-John's-wort to restore her strength. Several years later, when an orthopedic surgeon from Germany examined Madame Zoya's ankle he declared that it looked like the work of a veterinarian, the kind of job one would expect to see on a household pet. For years, slivers of metal continued to work their way through Madame Zoya's skin.

At the beginning of her convalescence she fell into a panic when she realized that there was no one to take care of her. She was isolated in an apartment building full of drug-dealing strangers and she didn't know where to get help. Most of her friends had died or moved away and her only relatives did not want to become involved. One nephew told her, "We warned you to move out of that building years ago, but you wouldn't listen." One day there was a soft knock on the door. Madame Zoya hobbled down the narrow hallway. She peeked through the spy hole and saw a tall, well-groomed Hispanic man whom she did not recognize.

"And who are you?" said Madame Zoya.

"Roberto," the man said.

"I do not know a Roberto," said Madame Zoya from her side of the door.

"Yes you do. You are my little Russian princess," he said. "Please open the door for me, Zoey."

Not knowing what to expect, Madame Zoya unlocked the door and opened it.

"*Abuela!* [Grandmother!]" the man exclaimed. "We have not seen you on the street. Is everything all right with you?" Madame Zoya stood there for a moment before she recognized him. Roberto had grown up in the apartment building and she remembered him from his childhood.

Roberto ran the drug-dealing operation on the street. He lived in a respectable neighborhood in one of the outer boroughs and only came to the neighborhood from time to time to take care of business. As a little boy he had called Madame Zoya the little Russian princess because of her diminutive size. Madame Zoya sat down at the kitchen table with Roberto and cried. She showed him her ankle and described the plain facts of her situation. Roberto listened and then told her not to worry. He would take care of her. Roberto hired a woman in the building to help Madame Zoya. Her name was Martine, and Roberto told her to clean the apartment once a week, and do the daily food shopping, laundry, ironing and anything else that needed to be done. At the end of Martine's first day, Madame Zoya offered to pay the woman, but she refused to take her money. Martine simply dismissed the offer with a wave of her hand and said, "Roberto." Young men from the street dropped by from time to time to take out the garbage and to ask if Madame Zoya needed anything.

"I must be honest with you," Madame Zoya told me. "Some of the peoples here are like savages from the jungle. They drink. They take I don't know what drugs and sometimes make toilet in the hallway. They fight and sometimes they kill each other for television set. But Roberto and Martine? They are like angels to me."

Two years after the automobile accident Madame Zoya was savagely attacked in the elevator by a woman who tried to take her gold crucifix, wedding ring and wallet. Madame Zoya was determined that no one was going to take her wedding ring. The woman would have to kill her for it. Madame Zoya cried out for help, but the elevator went up and down four times without anyone responding. The woman raked Madame Zoya's face with her fingernails and bloodied her mouth and nose with her fists. Madame Zoya lay on the floor of the elevator unable to defend herself. The woman kicked her in the stomach, the legs, and then broke her bad ankle. When Madame Zoya saw the metal pin in her ankle protruding through her flesh, she thought it was the end—that the woman was going to kill her.

The elevator shuddered to a stop on one of the upper floors. The door banged open to reveal the silhouette of a man standing by himself. It was Roberto. Without a word, he grabbed the woman by the hair and dragged her from the elevator. He beat her unconscious and then pounded her head on the floor.

"Please, Roberto! No!" Madame Zoya pleaded from the floor of the elevator. "You are going to kill her."

"Are you crazy, *abuela*? She was ready to kill you."

"Well then, if you are going to kill her, please don't do it in front of me. I couldn't bear it."

Roberto left the woman unconscious on the floor and then drove Madame Zoya to the hospital where a surgeon repaired her ankle. After Madame Zoya returned to the apartment, Martine came every day to take care of her. By that time, Roberto had put out the word to everyone in the building and on the street that Madame Zoya was "family" and under his protection. This incident happened years before I met Madame Zoya, but during my visits to her apartment to learn about Russian cooking, young men or women sometimes arrived unexpectedly at her front door, nice as can be, carrying groceries or folded laundry.

I continued to visit Madame Zoya every month, and in her kitchen she taught me how to make caviar from fresh roe, and the proper way to prepare gravlax with boned salmon fillets, white pepper, salt, sugar and a handful of fresh dill that we bruised on the countertop with our fists. The day we baked a lingonberry tart called kisel, we drank Armenian brandy and listened to an album of Russian gypsy music by Zina Vishnevskaya and Gueorgui Parthogh. "Zina . . . ah, Zina!" Madame Zoya said. "Now you listen close, because this woman she sing from her heart." She got up to bring me a serving of kisel from the counter and as she moved across the kitchen floor she held out her arms and danced a few steps while humming to herself. I poured out another measure of brandy and she had me write down her vague directions to L'Etoile de Moscou, a small Russian restaurant in Paris, where she had dined thirty-five years earlier. Then she described, in luscious detail, the flavor of a sweet plum she once ate during a childhood summer on the Black Sea.

On a different visit, she told me how to hunt for wild ginseng at night, and where to buy the best herring in the five boroughs (at a small store on the corner of 76th Street and Northern Parkway in Queens). I wrote down a folk remedy to cure bronchitis (hot milk mixed with a tablespoon of lard and honey with a pinch of baking soda), and another for the treatment for burns, but then it was time to go. I was drunk, the neighborhood was growing unsettled, and I wanted to leave the building before dark. While I waited for the bus, I promised myself never to come back to the neighborhood because I felt it was only a matter of time before something bad happened to me.

On my next visit I brought Madame Zoya a loaf of black rye bread, a dozen eggs, cream and smoked herring from a delicatessen on the Lower East Side. Along, of course, with a bottle of Russian vodka. Considering her powers of persuasion, I was grateful I hadn't met Madame Zoya when she was a young woman. I knew it wasn't safe to visit her and that it would make far better sense for me to pay her cab fare to come teach me how to cook in my own kitchen on the Upper East Side. But in the end, I realized the mood wouldn't be right in a different setting and so I continued to make the long journeys to her Washington Heights apartment. I survived these visits and, considering the possibilities for violence, everything went well. Madame Zoya doled out her knowledge of cooking and life in such a way that there was always some unfinished detail of a recipe, or part of an anecdote left untold in order to draw me back for more. I began to get an uneasy feeling that for years to come I would be seduced into traveling uptown to Madame Zoya's on a regular basis, with bags full of groceries. At some point I started calling her Zoey rather than Madame Zoya.

During the course of these visits, the neighborhood started to change. Or maybe it was my attitude that shifted. Probably a little of both. The men on the street stopped offering me drugs and I developed that special New York City mind-set of being invisible. Few of the men on the street and in Zoey's building made eye contact with me, and I did everything I could to avoid it with them. Then one day a hulking stranger came up to me and stood in the middle of the sidewalk, blocking my way. There was no avoiding him and just as I was preparing for the worst, he asked if Madame Zoya needed anything.

Not all of my visits were happy ones. I arrived one day to find her crying at the table with blistered burns on her chest and forearm. An eggplant had exploded as she took it from the oven. I helped clean her up and poured two small measures of vodka to lift her spirits. Typical of her optimism, she said she was grateful the eggplant hadn't blown up in her face.

With the exception of gravlax, I don't have many occasions to prepare most of the dishes that Zoey taught me. But whenever I see rolled pickled herring at a delicatessen counter

I think to myself, "Zoey could do better." Nearly every recipe that I collect holds the memory of a person or a place or a moment in time. Practically all of my Russian recipes remind me of Zoey and the conversations that took place on the particular day she taught me each dish.

I left New York City and moved back to California. I thought about Zoey often, but I only called her once on Russian Christmas to wish her a happy holiday and to see how she was doing. "Well," she said, "I can tell you this: I am still here on this good earth." She asked when I would come for another visit. She sounded older but in good spirits, and we talked about what we would prepare for our lunch. I suspect that both of us knew we would never see each other again, but we couldn't say it because we didn't want to believe all of those times were in the past.

Before we got off the phone I asked Zoey if she was afraid of living by herself. "No," she said. "I am not afraid because I know what it means to love life and survive. People with no belief and no faith and no hope are like empty box. They have nothing. Miracles happen every day. You think red tulip growing from black soil is not a miracle? I have my health and my memories and I thank God for my friends and for every day of my life."

THE BIRD MAN AND THE
LAP DANCER

WILDLIFE BIOLOGIST OLIVER SPARROW drives a 1992 Buick Roadmaster Dynaride. He lives in the Central Valley of California, where he conducts species surveys, habitat mapping, and conservation easements on private land. He is well known for his work on the Valley Elderberry Longhorn Beetle, the shorebird colonies in the municipal sewage ponds of the Central Valley, and, most recently, for a new sighting of the official California State Mollusk, *Ariolimax columbianus*, the one-footed, slime-producing, hermaphroditic terrestrial gastropod commonly known as the banana slug.

I first heard of Oliver at a dinner party in 1998 when one of the guests told a story about how Oliver had taken a group of strippers and lap dancers to look at the wintering Sandhill Cranes just north of Sacramento. Oliver was described as a jovial, fairly heavyset man of average height, with a round face and ruddy complexion, curly ginger-colored hair and a pleasant disposition. Naturally, everyone at the table wondered how the trip had come about and especially what possible interest the dancers would have in Oliver Sparrow or the Sandhill Cranes and other migratory birds of the Pacific Flyway.

At the end of dinner I got Oliver's work number. I was told he was in his mid-forties and that he lived with his mother, who was confined to a wheelchair and in poor health. Three years later, when I finally got around to calling him at work to discuss bird-watching, Elderberry Longhorn Beetles, banana slugs and strippers he agreed to talk to me if I promised not to tell his mother about the girls.

FIRST MEETING WITH OLIVER SPARROW

We met after work at a small blues club in a seedy part of downtown Sacramento. In keeping with his interest in birds, Oliver ordered a double shot of Wild Turkey and I had the same. He told me he had 454 bird species on his life list and that he specialized in what is known as auditory birding, identification by song and call. His most recently confirmed species sighting was a Grasshopper Sparrow in the Yolo Bypass, which is the floodwater drainage area for the Sacramento and American rivers. We chatted for a while and from what I could gather, Oliver was in the habit of spending many of his lunch breaks and early evening hours at a local topless club called Heart Breakers. As he warmed to the subject he described how one evening a dancer by the name of Sindy asked him what he did for a living. He told her he was a wildlife biologist.

"Vertebrate or invertebrate?" she said.

"Vertebrate . . . mostly birds," Oliver replied. "But I also dabble in invertebrates from time to time depending on the client. Slugs and bugs, you know. Mapping their habitats and counting them . . . and some behavioral observations about mating."

"You make a living counting slugs and watching them have sex?" she said.

"Well, yeah, sort of . . . as a sideline," Oliver explained. "But not for pay. Just fun stuff."

"Fun stuff?" she said.

As it turned out, Sindy (her stage name) had been interested in hawks since her childhood on the outskirts of Chicago. Her mother was an avid backyard birder and she nurtured Sindy's interest in identifying different species and observing their behavior. In her off-hours Sindy volunteered at the Sacramento Science Center, helping to rehabilitate hawks and other injured raptors. During the day, she worked as a nurse at the nearby Sutter Hospital. When Oliver asked her about the odd juxtaposition of jobs, nursing and stripping, she said that dealing with the off-duty doctors at Heart Breakers in the evenings and getting leered at and groped by them at the surgical center during the days wasn't all that much of a switch.

When Oliver wasn't at Heart Breakers watching the dancers or talking with them about natural history and wildlife, he worked for clients such as the Nature Conservancy. In the winter of 2002, shortly before I first met him, Oliver was conducting a waterfowl survey when he stumbled upon a new population of banana slugs on Staten island in the Sacramento

River Delta. They were found low down by the water on the levee riprap. Banana slugs had not been previously reported from the Central Valley or the Delta and it was thought that their local haunts were confined to the coastal redwood forests and a few isolated pockets in the moist woodlands in the foothills of the Sierra Nevada. "It's not often that one finds critters so far out of their known range and habitat," Oliver told me. At the time of his discovery, there were no known banana slug populations within thirty-five miles of Staten island, and so Oliver decided to report his finding to Dr. Janet Leonard, one of the world's preeminent malacologists, at the University of California–Santa Cruz. In his e-mail to Dr. Leonard, he invited her to come see his "thundering herd of banana slugs."

Dr. Leonard drove to Staten island to have a look at Oliver's slugs and to collect a few specimens for DNA analysis in order to determine the species. They looked like *Ariolimax columbianus*, but she decided to wait for the results of the lab work before making a positive identification. Oliver told me that Dr. Leonard's work on the three species and two subspecies of banana slug was primarily focused on reassessing the phylogeny, taxonomy and biogeography of the genus *Ariolimax*, but that she was probably far better known for her research on the bizarre mating behavior of banana slugs. Oliver gave me her telephone number and shortly after I contacted Dr. Leonard, she sent me several of her research papers to give me an overview of her work. Even the dry, clinical facts of banana slug courtship, foreplay and sex, as observed under laboratory conditions, were mesmerizing; and with the help of Alice Bryant Harper's pamphlet, "The Banana Slug: A Close Look at a Giant Forest Slug of Western North America," I finally caught the drift of why Oliver Sparrow, Dr. Leonard and so many other people were captivated by banana slugs.

That first night, Oliver told me about banana slug penises. According to Harper, the scientific names of one species and one subspecies refer solely to penis length, nomenclature which might be unique in the field of taxonomy. *Ariolimax dolichophallus* means the banana slug with the big penis, and the subspecies *Ariolimax californicus brachyphallus* describes the banana slug with the short penis. But, as Oliver pointed out, this distinction between "big" and "short" was hardly worth thinking about because the penises of all banana slugs are about the same length as their bodies, which are typically six to ten inches long.

"Incredibly sexy critters," Oliver explained. "Fossil record isn't clear, because of the soft-tissue problem, but it is hypothesized that slugs evolved from marine snails that went ashore during the Devonian period, about 400 million years ago. They use their radula, a tongue-like organ with 27,000 tiny teeth, to arouse their potential mates. Their penises are located on their heads. At a certain point they start to wave them in the air as some sort of courtship display. It is quite a sight. Foreplay lasts for hours as they circle each other in a clockwise direction—licking, nibbling and rasping at each other's genital region. They taste and eat each other's slime; maybe to get turned on, or as some sort of exchange of genetic information. When sufficiently aroused, they enter each other and have continuous sex for up to thirty-six hours. If a suitable mate isn't available they can have sex with themselves."

"I would expect nothing less of the official California State Mollusk," I said.

To redirect the conversation and ease our way into the topic of bird-watching with topless dancers, I asked Oliver to fill me in on some of the highlights of his career as a wildlife biologist.

"Well, my first endangered species sighting took place in 1986 in Bakersfield, California," he said. "I was pulling into the parking lot of a discount liquor store in a shopping mall one night when the headlights of my car suddenly illuminated a San Joaquin Kit Fox, *Vulpes macrotis*. It was jumping out of a dumpster with a plastic-wrapped sandwich in its mouth and a radio-tracking collar around its neck."

"Sounds like a good example of species survival through adaptation," I said.

"I know what you mean about adaptation, but its new habitat and feeding behavior sort of took some of the romance out of the sighting."

In 1987 Oliver was hired by the renowned ornithologist Jarad Verner to help with a project to standardize bird census techniques for the U.S. Fish and Wildlife Service. Most ornithologists in the field have inherent habits of observation, known as "bias," that affect their ability to accurately count bird species and estimate their relative numbers. The purpose of the study was to identify and hopefully minimize personal bias. Oliver told me that his own personal bias had to do with his difficulty in hearing low-frequency calls of birds such as the Blue Grouse and Great Horned Owl. Not long after he completed his work for Verner, Oliver decided to drive from California to Maine in order to conduct an informal survey of birds. During that cross-country trip he took a special interest in Colima Warblers, Montezuma Quail, Harris's Hawk and long-distance neotropical migrants such as the Western Tanager and Wilson's Warbler.

"I learned a lot on that trip," Oliver told me, "but the deciduous forest warblers were a fucking nightmare. Dense woodlands, at least thirty different species all mixed together in the upper levels of the trees, and few visual clues. In three hours I nailed less than ten species. Pathetic."

Oliver Sparrow has also worked for the U.S. Forest Service, near Bucks Lake in Plumas County, where he counted a mountain thrush known as Townsend's Solitaire, Spotted Owls, and the rarely seen Northern Goshawk near Oroville. On Goodyear Creek, near Downieville, California, Oliver met a retired construction worker by the name of Cyrus Rollins who was a self-taught expert on the flora and fauna and natural history of the local area. Rollins knew all the scientific names of the plants and animals, and his soft-spoken manner and passion and his insight into wildlife habitat and natural biotic communities had a lasting influence on Oliver's work as a biologist. Among other skills, Cyrus taught Oliver the fine art of determining where and when ladybugs congregate, in order to collect and sell them to biological pest control companies and local nurseries.

Another one of Oliver's mentors was Larry Salata, a lab instructor for a very influential birder by the name of Miklos Udvardy who worked in the Department of Biological

Sciences at California State University–Sacramento. "Larry Salata was partially color-blind," Oliver told me, "but he was a wizard at identifying birds by call and song, and he's the one who taught me how to do it myself."

Oliver talked about waterfowl migration, the Burrowing Owl, *Athene cunicularia*, and his membership in a local dragonfly watchers club. He discussed the upcoming Pacific Flyway Duck Calling Championships, and the positive and negative influences of agricultural crops and flood control on wildlife patterns and habitat use. Oliver referred to the Elderberry Longhorn Beetle as "woodpecker candy." He also told me that over short distances banana slugs had been clocked at speeds in excess of .007 miles per hour. When I asked him why nesting shorebirds were attracted to the municipal sewage ponds of the Central Valley he said the ponds were nutrient-rich and that the birds didn't really care where the nutrients came from. Oliver described his recent work on the Golden Gate Bridge in San Francisco as part of a "seabird shit abatement program." The main concern was worker safety, because of slippery walkways and hand railings, but there was also the issue of protecting the structural integrity of the towers from the corrosive effects of bird guano. I didn't ask him to elaborate on this little-known threat to the bridge, and after several more shots of Wild Turkey our conversation finally came around to how Oliver became a regular patron of Heart Breakers.

"To celebrate my third-of-a-century birthday party— (thirty-three and a third years), a colleague took me to the club for lunch. That first visit was more of a joke than anything else. I had never been to a topless strip club, or anything like it, and I was a little uneasy about walking into such a place, especially in broad daylight in the middle of the week. I didn't know what to expect, but Heart Breakers turned out to be a small, friendly, easygoing neighborhood place where a lot of people knew each other. The club served alcohol and offered a limited menu. The elevated stage ended at a bar top and tipping rail. Five girls were working the day shift and one of them introduced me to her mother and sister who had come to watch her at work. The dancers were officially hired as cocktail waitresses and probably got paid minimum wage, but they made most of their money on tips. No nudity, just stripping and topless dancing. Officially, it wasn't a hands-on sort of place, but there was a back room for lap dancing. I had mixed feelings about going to Heart Breakers, but it got me to thinking about what it all meant."

"What do you mean by 'what it all meant'?" I asked.

"Well, the girls were gorgeous, funny, and sexy, but it was kinda weird because the ones I talked to were smart. I just wasn't expecting them to be smart. They were also friendly and direct and I think that this is part of what drew me into the world of topless dancers. I also liked their eccentric ways and how they had no qualms about speaking their minds or talking freely about sex. I never meant to become a regular, but I went back a couple of times on my own and before I knew it, I was on the Heart Breakers softball team.

"The team was made up of guys who hung out at the club. It was a ragtag group that included an electrician, a defense attorney, a wine merchant, a greengrocer, a baker, a fireman and a few mystery guys who we weren't quite sure what they did for a living. We were coached by a prison guard who worked at the Vacaville State Medical Facility. This is a nice term for the place where they take inmates from the state prison system who are not well mentally.

"Our softball team was pathetic. We lost all of our games except for the one when the other team didn't show up. But no other team in the league had a rooting section like ours. Wall-to-wall babes from Heart Breakers cheering us on to our every defeat. All of the dancers had stage names, and they gave most of their regular customers nicknames. Mine was 'Bird Man,' and I can still remember stepping up to the plate and hearing the girls yelling, 'Go, Bird Man!' It was a lot of fun. After the games the team took the girls out for drinks. I know this is going to sound strange, but the girls liked us. We would cheer for them and shout encouragement while they were on stage dancing and taking off their clothes, and they would do the same for us when we were out there on the softball field."

"So what led up to the first bird-watching field trip?" I said.

"Well, one of our 'star players' on the softball team suddenly died of a heart attack at home. He was young—in his late thirties. He didn't have any family to take care of the funeral arrangements, so one of the other customers and the girls organized a wake in his honor. About twenty girls from the club showed up. It turned into a pretty raucous evening and at one point Sindy and another woman, Kara, asked me if I would take them out to look at the Greater Sandhill Cranes that I had been telling them about at the club. This seemed like a good idea at the time, but it wasn't long before I ran into all sorts of problems with their boyfriends. These guys wanted to beat the shit out of me. They just couldn't get their minds around the Sandhill Crane–viewing story. And the management at Heart Breakers made it real clear about their rules prohibiting clients and dancers from socializing after hours. They were legitimately worried about losing their license because of the prostitution issue. The strange thing was that the guys didn't care about their girlfriends stripping or lap dancing for me. It was a friendly professional exchange in a safe place with a bouncer standing by. But taking the girls to a remote area to watch birds was definitely viewed as suspect and possibly deviant behavior. They must have thought I was some kind of pervert. A lot of these guys are abusive and violent and unpredictable and in their minds stripping, lap dancing and bird-watching just didn't add up to anything good."

Everyone eventually calmed down and the first field trip took place about thirty miles north of Sacramento at the Gray Lodge State Wildlife Area, near the Sutter Buttes. The area is managed mainly for wintering waterfowl, but there is also a section of land set aside for hunters. The area is a complex of freshwater marshes, creeks with riparian habitat, and grasslands that provide an ideal roosting area for waterfowl. Oliver and the girls got off to a late start because Sindy and Kara had worked the night before, but by eleven A.M. they arrived at the Gray Lodge parking lot. As they stepped out of Oliver's car, they made their first confirmed species sighting: *Homo sapiens*—a group of drunken duck hunters on their way home. The hunters were decked out in camouflage clothing and they carried guns. Oliver was nervous because he was in such a remote area with two beautiful women.

"Maybe we should wait here in the parking lot until they leave," Oliver suggested.

"Fuckwits," Sindy said. "Loaded guns, alcohol and testosterone. We have to deal with this shit at the club all the time. Don't worry. If they get any funny ideas, Kara and I will handle it."

Kara was more concerned about what the wind and rain would do to her hair. The hunters looked at Oliver, dressed in his knee-high rubber boots, binoculars around his neck, and a bird-watcher's vest with its mind-boggling array of pockets to suit every purpose. The hunters checked out the girls, mumbled the usual derogatory comments to each other and then opened a few more beers as they packed their trucks. The men drove off and within a short while Oliver had set up his spotting scope and was busy rattling off the common names of different waterfowl. He described the day as being cold, wet and blustery, and so I asked Oliver what the two women wore for the field trip.

"No thongs . . . just regular clothes," he said.

According to Oliver, the field trip went well. The girls loved the offbeat adventure and they were thrilled by his knowledge of birds and other wildlife. They saw wintering Greater Sandhill Cranes, plus clouds of Snow Geese with their distinctive black wing tips. There were Greater White-fronted Geese, mallards, American and Eurasian Wigeons, Northern Pintail Ducks, and various raptors. They watched stately Great Blue Herons and Great Egrets foraging for amphibians, fish and small rodents.

"As it turned out," Oliver told me, "Kara had a great eye for finding birds and her observational skills were really impressive. She even nailed the Red-Shouldered Hawk, *Buteo lineatus,* in a eucalyptus tree and that really knocked my socks off."

"So what did the girls think of the field trip?" I said.

"They thought it was a bit weird, but interesting. A crazy thing to do because most dancers avoid associating with customers outside of the club. They make a very clear distinction between their work and their private lives. I'm still not sure why, but a lot of the girls trusted me and they let me step into their daily lives as a friend. I've visited their kids when they were sick in the hospital, I sometimes help them go shopping for outfits for the club, but I think my real value is that I can sit quietly and listen to them when they need someone to talk to. Their lives are pretty complicated and many of them have been physically and emotionally damaged by men. The field trip to Gray Lodge was probably the turning point for me. From that day on, the word was out that 'Bird Man' was OK."

Late that afternoon, Oliver took Sindy and Kara back to Sacramento so they could get ready for their night shift at Heart Breakers. Oliver drove home by himself. He walked into the house just in time to get dinner ready for his mother.

"Did you have a nice afternoon bird-watching with your friends?" she asked.

"Yes, Mom," he said.

On a second field trip, a few months later, Oliver took two other dancers, Amber and Leyla, to look at wildflowers at the Jepson Prairie Nature Preserve. Jepson Prairie has one of the largest remaining claypan vernal pools and native bunchgrass prairie habitats in northern California. A vernal pool is a type of seasonal wetland, usually a wide, shallow body of water that perches above an impenetrable soil layer of clay or rock. As the pool recedes, due to evaporation, concentric rings of different-colored wildflowers come into bloom. The day of the wildflower trip they saw rings of yellow Buttercups, white Meadow Foam, blue Dowingia, yellow-white Tidy Tips, purple Blue Dicks, and white Popcorn Flowers. Not too many birds were out that day, but Oliver managed to spot several grassland species and a Pacific Tree Frog. After about three hours of wildflower viewing, they sat down in a grove of nonnative Blue Gum Eucalyptus, where they drank a couple of bottles of wine and looked at the Great Blue Heron rookery near the parking lot.

JOURNEY TO COLD CANYON
WITH OLIVER SPARROW

By the time Oliver and I managed to set aside time for a field trip, the wildflowers were finished, and winter birding had tapered off. Kara was eight months pregnant, Leyla's little daughter was in intensive care, Sindy was only interested in raptors—and so that pretty well precluded the possibility of going on a field trip with Oliver and the dancers. But I wanted to see Oliver in his element so, with few other options, Oliver suggested that we do a bit of late-spring general birding and then look around for banana slugs in a place called Stebbens Cold Canyon Reserve. Cold Canyon is a narrow riparian corridor which forms part of the drainage system for the Vaca Mountains, on the eastern slope of California's Inner Coast Range.

We arrived at the trailhead of Cold Canyon early one morning and headed upstream on a well-worn pathway. Within minutes, Oliver started making a series of strange-sounding "pish . . . pish . . . pish" calls. He referred to the sounds as "pishing"—which is a general-purpose, broad-frequency mobbing call to attract the attention of multiple bird species. Before long, the birds were calling back and Oliver started to identify them.

"Oak Titmouse, *Baeolophus inornatus*. A plain Jane for sure, but the sucker has fifteen songs and calls. And, hey, check it out! Bachelor California Quail calling for hot babes. Yep . . . and that's the Spotted Towhee. And over to the left . . . There! Hear that mewing call? That's the Blue Gray Gnatcatcher. OK, and now that's a Wren Tit. Very pair-oriented and territorial. Can you hear the distinctive 'Ping-Pong ball bouncing to a stop on top of a table' voice of the male? And that's a Bush Tit—the ultimate flocking bird. Hear that 'tik, tik, tik' sound? Those are contact calls. Bush Tits are team-oriented and very insecure. They like to be in constant contact with the rest of the flock. Especially the little baby Bush Tits."

"Hey, Oliver, there seem to be a lot of tits out this morning," I joked, and no sooner were these words out of my mouth than a young man and woman appeared on the trail. Walking in front, the woman wore a tight tank top that just barely contained a shapely set of firm, full breasts. With beach towels and a picnic hamper in hand, the couple was obviously headed upstream for one of the secluded, rock-lined, clear-water swimming holes that Oliver had told me about.

"Nice upper canopy," muttered Oliver, after the couple passed us. "Looks like the female of the species appreciates a good riparian live oak woodland on a sunny day. Won't be long before she's naked. And down there in the river, next winter and early spring, California newts will be crawling all over the place . . . breeding like bunnies."

Oliver pointed to something crawling on the ground. "Uggh, Velvet Ant," he said. "A nasty little predator. There are at least thirty-three different ant species in Cold Canyon, but this is one of the few that I know."

We didn't find a single banana slug that day. Oliver thought it was too hot and dry for the slugs to be roaming about during daylight hours. On our way back to the car, we stopped at the spot where Oliver made a banana slug sighting in 1988. "It was right here, during a birding trip with a group from the local Audubon Society," Oliver told me, as he pointed to a cool, damp, shaded area at the side of the trail. "Just by coincidence, we happened upon a banana slug as it was exiting a discarded banana skin that it had been feeding on. As the birders gathered around me, I said, 'Oh, now here is something interesting—the banana slug *Ariolimax columbianus* just emerging from its egg case.'" Oliver laughed when he told me that a few of the people took careful notes to document this rare sighting.

When we got back to where Oliver had parked his Buick Roadmaster, at the bottom of Cold Canyon, I asked him if he ever had sex with the dancers.

"Two out of twenty-eight," he replied without hesitation, "but they weren't friends so it was OK. We just got carried away."

I am still uncertain what he meant by this statement, but I suspect he felt it wasn't quite right to have sex with female friends or other women he knew too well.

ANCIENT ANTS, THE CURRENT IN THE RIVER, AND THE DIVINE PATHWAY

Several months later Oliver arranged for us to have dinner with Leyla. I wanted to see Oliver with one of his dancer friends in a neutral place, away from the club, in order to have a better idea of their connection. Oliver and I arrived at the restaurant early. We went to the bar and I selected a seat where I could watch the front door. Dozens of men and women moved through the lobby, but when Leyla walked in the door, fifteen minutes later, I immediately knew she was the one. Her posture and walk conveyed a demure, self-assured feminine presence. Leyla was in her early thirties with medium-length brunette hair, a soft, silky, flawless complexion and an easy smile. Her light touch of makeup and hint of perfume perfectly complemented her natural beauty. Everything about her appearance and demeanor and the way she dressed was modest and understated in a very attractive sort of way.

Once we were seated, Oliver opened the conversation with a story about Argentine Ants. He told us how the tiny black ants arrived in Southern California around 1891 in shiploads of sugar from Argentina, and then went on to explain how this nonnative ant species, *Linepithema humile*, had successfully invaded the entire length of California to form a continuous supercolony that extended from San Diego to southern Oregon. Quoting from an article published in *Conservation Biology*, Oliver told us how the colony was growing at a rate of about 650 feet per year and that the Argentine Ants were wreaking havoc on the indigenous ant species of the Central Valley, such as the Valley Oak Ant and the Ancient Ant. The overwhelming biomass of the super-colony was also contributing to the decline of the coastal horned lizards because the lizards would not eat the Argentine Ants that had displaced the larger and more palatable native ant species.

"What are Ancient Ants?" Leyla asked.

"The Ancient Ant, *Smithistruma reliquia*, is a below-surface-feeding ant," Oliver explained. "It is known only from one location near the intersection of County Road 17 and State Highway 113, about four kilometers east of the town of Yolo and north of the city of Woodland. It appears to be a primitive and relic species from when the region was much wetter. It is rare and in serious decline from the loss and disturbance of riparian habitat in the Central Valley. Nearly 95 percent of California's riparian habitats have been destroyed for agriculture, development and flood control. In addition to climatic change and habitat loss, the Argentine Ant competes with and destroys native ant species. In other words, the Ancient Ant is probably fucked."

"What do Ancient Ants look like?" said Leyla.

"If you look inside their mouth, under a microscope, you will see a really cool baleenlike structure, similar to whales', which is quite unlike other ants."

"How do you catch an Ancient Ant?" I asked.

"Well, they live in leaf litter so we have to use a Winkler separator to capture them," Oliver explained.

"A Winkler separator?" said Leyla.

"It's actually called a photoeclector or, more properly, a Winkler/Moczarki Elector. We use them out in the field. First you presift the soil or leaf litter onto a screen in a darkened container and then close the top. At the bottom of the container, below the screen, is a funnel that leads to a clear glass collecting jar with a moist cloth at the bottom. The ants are attracted to the light and humidity in the collecting jar," Oliver told us.

"Are you interested in insects?" I asked Leyla.

"Not really," she laughed, "I just didn't want Oliver to get started on banana slugs again."

The waitress came back to our table for the fourth time in twenty minutes to politely inquire if we were ready to order our dinner. None of us had looked at the menus, but now we made our choices and when the waitress left I asked Leyla how she got into dancing.

"I originally started dancing to pay off medical bills from a car accident, and a college loan. I have a degree in English literature with a minor in philosophy from St. Mary's College. To become a dancer, first you go in to be interviewed. This is just for the club owner to see what you look like. Then you come back for the live ten-minute audition in front of customers. For me, the audition was midday at Heart Breakers. I was so nervous I thought I was going to throw up just before I went on. Auditions are usually terrible, but I made $38 in tips my first time onstage and that was a club record that stood for two years. But once I felt comfortable about being up on stage, in front of strangers, I discovered that dancing topless is all about power and controlling that power. About finding self-confidence; learning to walk within the rules of the club, and the law, and knowing what is safe with the clients. You are competing for tips against the other four dancers on your shift, but you can't let jealousy or anger with your coworkers develop. After I dug myself out of debt, I kept dancing because I wanted to buy a house. I saved my money for three years. Then I got married and had a baby. I stopped working at the club about three years ago. The dance money made it possible for me to stay at home with my little girl. Sometimes I do bachelor parties and private shows for clients like Oliver as long as I know who I'm dealing with. I don't take chances with strangers and I never take all of my clothes off."

"What does your husband think about your dancing?" I said.

"He's fine with it. But you have to understand that he is a fairly complex character himself. He was brought up as a Seventh-Day Adventist and his family didn't believe in regular dancing. He works as a graphic designer and is the lead singer in a punk rock band. When we were dating he used to come in to watch me at Heart Breakers, but I had to make it clear that I couldn't come over and cuddle up to him at the bar, because I was at work. I was a stripper when we first met so the decision about getting involved with me was his choice. My husband wants to hit the big time as a singer. He is on the road with his band most of the time. In many ways I feel like a single mom, but I had to accept what he did for a living. One thing I have learned is that you can't stifle a person's dreams and then expect things to work out. Life isn't like that."

At some point, dinner was brought to the table, but we merely picked at the food as we continued to talk. Oliver told us how a huge taxonomic battle was still being fought in the birding world because of a genetic study that had moved turkey vultures into New World storks. "That was one gutsy move," Oliver pointed out, "and long overdue, in my opinion. The proper designation was disputed for over twenty years and finally resolved, for most of us, in the 1990s." Leyla continued her description of what it was like to be a topless dancer and it was at about this point in the evening that I began to notice how people at the adjoining tables were trying to follow our disjointed conversation.

"Dancing helped me discover myself as a sexual being and how to recognize and harness my own power as a woman," said Leyla. "I have a drop-dead beautiful mother who is only seventeen years older than me. In high school, my boyfriends would come over to visit, and all they wanted to do was look at my mother. It made me feel insecure and inadequate. It was as if I could never measure up to her. I was brought up as a good Catholic girl. I was always a very shy and modest person, but onstage I became Aphrodite for six hours. Everyone wanted me, both men and women. You feel the power and it makes you high. I learned to be proud of my body and to be in control of it. I also learned to trust my feelings about people, both good and bad feelings, and to follow my instincts."

"Following instincts?" Oliver laughed. "More like survival of the fittest. Tell the story about Large Marge and about the night you threw your shoe."

"OK. Both stories are good examples of responding to the moment. There was a big lesbian who came into the club from time to time. We nicknamed her Large Marge. So Marge was sitting at the tipping rail. Just drinking quietly, peeling off a few bills for the dancers and minding her own business. At the end of my set I used to get down on my knees, wearing only a pair of skimpy panties, with my back to the customers, and then leaned backward until my head was right where people put their drinks. Women customers can be much more unpredictable than the guys. The next thing I knew, Marge had me pinned to the bar top in a lip lock with her tongue in my mouth. I was trapped in that position and Marge wasn't in any hurry to let go. Everyone at the tipping rail went crazy. I was mad and insulted, but I didn't let it show. I made a joke out of it, and in return for keeping my cool people showered the dance floor with money. Another night, and Oliver saw this, there was a bachelor party that staggered in just before midnight. The guys were really drunk and saying a lot of mean things to the dancers. I had just pulled off my tank top and bra when a man stood up, lifted his T-shirt over his face and said, 'Hey, Leyla, I can shake my titties, too.' Without thinking, I took off one of my heavy platform shoes and threw it at him as hard as I could. He didn't see it coming and somehow the shoe hit him square in the forehead and knocked him out. The music stopped and the room went dead silent. The bouncer instinctively moved toward the stage in case someone tried to hurt me. But, once again, I had done the right thing. The crowd erupted in laughter and started throwing hundreds of dollars at me. I broke a thousand dollars that night. A dancer could never plan moments like these, but if you are good, you learn to take advantage of these opportunities.

"Getting back to what I was talking about earlier, dancing helped me to discover and develop who I am. Not just onstage, but the person I am in everyday life. My real name is Susan, but my stage name is Leyla. Part of the process of being a successful dancer has to do with finding the character within yourself, but I think the most important thing to learn about dancing is how to become the perfect reflection of the customer's fantasy. I am proud of my skill. It is like being a courtesan or a geisha. You must know yourself, know your client, and you must always be in control."

"What was it like when you first started out?" I asked.

"Dancing was the chrysalis state of discovering who I am. It was an extraordinary sensation to awaken to how I felt within my skin. Onstage I learned to let go, to purge myself of insecurity and self-doubt. Getting into character night after night and creating the illusion of intimacy with strangers was exhausting, but it also set off a profound outpouring of emotion for me. Of course, the customers couldn't tell what was going on in my mind. Good dancing is read as 'wanting' or 'needing.' This is what makes it sexy and what draws the customers in. What the customers see in your body language is vulnerability and hot desire. But you have to know how far to go with the titillation because you can't expect to mix money, men, naked women and alcohol and expect to have an easy time. There is a delicate balance between 'safe' and 'not safe,' but we always had a bouncer there to protect us if things got out of hand."

"The bouncers are there to minimize and contain the stupidity," Oliver explained.

"Sometimes it went way beyond the realm of stupidity," Leyla said. "One night a crazy customer knifed a trainee bouncer in the stomach. Our regular bouncer just took the guy apart. Demolished him. I had never seen anything like that. He dragged him out the door and dumped him in the parking lot. Then he called the ambulance for our guy and stayed with him to calm him down and keep him conscious. After the ambulance left, the management notified the police to come collect what was left of the knifer . . . which wasn't much."

I asked Leyla what went through her mind when she was onstage.

"I'm not thinking about doing the laundry. Onstage I'm focused on the music and my body. It's meditative. I can pour out emotions onstage without using words, but in everyday life I am very reserved. Each set is about ten to twelve minutes, the length of two or three songs. That means each girl is onstage about once an hour. There is a lot of unspoken interplay with the audience to build up energy and excitement during your set. As the songs progress, you take off a little bit more. I had many different 'looks' onstage, but whenever I dressed up as the 'Catholic schoolgirl gone bad' people flipped out. I wore a black-and-white checked, pleated skirt— very short—sometimes with white 'thigh-highs,' and either a cutoff white tank top that just covered my breasts, or a bra with a man's starched white dress shirt with the tails tied across my stomach. The simpler, the better. The white shirts with the buttoned-down collars came from Mervyn's, but they looked quite different when I wore them onstage. I also wore a pair of platform heels with blinking lights in the clear acrylic soles. They lit up with each step. Teasing and pleasing and making the customers want more is the name of this game. I would usually make $600 to $900 a shift, but one night in my schoolgirl outfit with the blinking shoes I took home $1600. Go figure."

Just as I asked Leyla how dancing had changed her, our waitress arrived at the table. Without interrupting our conversation, she stood there and listened to Leyla's reply.

"Topless dancing taught me to take chances and to do what I needed to do in my life. I am a very private person. I know this is going to sound strange, and maybe it has something to do with my Catholic upbringing, but dancing for me was a divine path that I followed. It was a blessing. Like finding the current in the river. Dancing and stripping helped me discover myself. My true self, not the person my friends and family saw. If it wasn't for the inner strength and self-confidence that dancing gave me, I could never survive what I am going through with my baby's health problems." Leyla placed a photo of her little girl on the tabletop for all of us to look at. "Oliver comes to the hospital to visit her on her bad days. He has an aging mother to take care of at home, so he knows what this is like."

"How is your little girl doing?" I said.

"She is OK right now. She's out of the hospital and back home."

"What happened to her?" I asked.

"She was born with a medical condition known as lymphedema that makes her extremely susceptible to infections. At birth, the doctors gave her a 1 percent chance of survival. She is three years old now and half her life has been spent in the hospital, most of that time in intensive care on a ventilator with me sleeping in a chair at the side of her bed. My husband and I think that if we can get her to age six she will have a chance. We need a miracle and that is what we pray for."

I reached across the table and touched the back of Leyla's hand. "I am sorry to hear that. Thank you for taking the time to come talk with me tonight."

"You're welcome," Leyla said.

The waitress blinked back tears and leaned forward to look at the photo as she asked us if everything was all right with our meal. After she left, Leyla answered more of my questions, and as she did so, I started to get an uneasy sensation in the pit of my stomach because the rest of the world was beginning to blur. For the second time, she "accidentally" brushed my leg with her foot. To say that she was charming and attentive and well spoken doesn't begin to do justice to the experience of talking to her and listening to her stories. They all seemed to come directly from her heart, unedited, original, mesmerizing, intelligent and spontaneous, but I also had a strong suspicion that she had prepared herself for the evening. She spoke in a normal, quiet voice but out of the corner of my eye I could see men straining to catch fragments of our conversation while still maintaining a semblance of interest at their own tables. Even men at the distant bar couldn't take their eyes off her. Our waitress hung on her every word as if Leyla held secret female knowledge about seduction, power and style.

I asked Leyla if she kept a journal or if she had ever considered writing about her experiences as a dancer. She told me she wrote in a daily diary she called her dance journal, but that she was far too self-conscious to let strangers look at her writing.

"Let me get this straight," I said. "You take off your clothes and dance for strangers for a living, but you feel that writing would expose you too much."

"Yes, that's right. There is something about the permanence of the written word that would make me feel too vulnerable. Good writing must come from the heart. For me to tell my story I would have to let complete strangers look into my soul and this is something that never happens in my profession."

That night we didn't confine our discussions to bugs and birds and naked women. We talked about "writer's voice," the tone and mood that make each good author's writing unique. Leyla asked me what I thought about gender bias in reading. I told her I wasn't sure such a thing existed, but that I had a pretty good example to support the theory. I admitted to keeping a Stihl chain-saw owner's manual with my bedside stack of *Atlantic Monthly* and *New Yorker* magazines. I asked Leyla for evidence of gender bias in her reading material and she confessed to owning a copy of *The Idiot Girl's Action Adventure Club* buried under *East of Eden, The Stone Diaries,* and *Papal Sin.* Leyla told us she had a special interest in the history of Catholicism. I was dubious, but when I asked her to explain the nature of this interest, she spoke at length about the influence of Aristotle's *Nicomachean Ethics* on St. Thomas

Aquinas, especially Thomas's writings on body and soul, and how this relates to the Resurrection. She went on to explain St. Thomas's philosophical synthesis of faith and reason in the Catholic Church. We also talked about the poet Rilke, the contribution of muses to twentieth-century literature and art, about physical desire and the emotional barriers that make it difficult for men and women to establish friendships of equality.

Without warning, Oliver suddenly let out a loud, deep call that sounded something like "kuk . . . kuk . . . keekeekee-keekeekeekuk . . . kuk!"

"I beg your pardon?" I said.

"The mating call of the Pileated Woodpecker—*Dryoco-pus pileatus*," Oliver explained. "Like a Northern Flicker on steroids."

"Impressive." Leyla laughed.

It was not the sort of evening I had anticipated. In order to draw Oliver back into the center of the conversation I asked him what he was working on. He told us about Dr. Leonard's work on sexual conflict and mating techniques of simultane-ously hermaphroditic gastropods, and about the lab tech-niques for banana slug DNA analysis. He wondered out loud about whether the procedure might simply require a small snippet of flesh, or if it might be necessary to mulch the entire slug in a blender as is commonly done with plants. "Quite frankly, the idea of pulping a banana slug makes me a bit queasy," he told us. I mentioned an infestation of scrub jays in my yard, and Oliver suspected that I might have the wrong kind of bird feeder. "Try a tube feeder for finches and use black oil sunflower seeds, or Niger thistle seeds," he said. "Should make all the difference in the world. I'll come over to check it out if you'd like me to."

When I asked Leyla what songs she preferred to dance to, she said that there were hundreds of songs she had used over the years. She mentioned songs from Def Leppard, Aerosmith, Melissa Etheridge, Marilyn Manson, the Rolling Stones and the Police. If it was a raucous night at Heart Breakers she loved to close down the place with "Friends in Low Places" by Garth Brooks. Some songs worked, others didn't, but what she searched for and eventually found was the sort of music that helped create what she called "magic moments" when the music, dancing and the audience became one.

"At Heart Breakers," Leyla said, "when a girl found a song that created this sense of magic . . . the song became 'hers' and the other dancers would usually acknowledge her right to that song. Sindy's signature song was 'Dream On' from a night she got up onstage, topless, barefoot, in a pair of skimpy cutoff Levi's with the front partially unbuttoned and did a dance that people are still talking about seven years later. No one touched the song after that. Some of the younger dancers didn't always respect or understand this unspoken proprietary right, and when they 'stole' a song the regular patrons and the other girls would respond to her performance with stony silence. If the dancer did it again she would be sent straight in the changing room."

"What are your signature songs?" I asked.

"There are quite a few. Most dancers and clubs like loud, hard 'power' music, but I almost always danced to softer music. 'Meltdown' from the soundtrack of *The Insiders* is a good example. It is sensuous and languid, with a pulsating beat like a heartbeat. It feels like really good slow sex to me and that's how I danced it. 'Give Me One Reason,' by Tracy Chapman; 'Pink,' by Aerosmith; and 'Wicked Game,' by Chris Isaak; all get a good reaction. Many of my favorite songs are ballads, but to make a song work it has to match a particular mood and a dancer's style. You create an illusion and hold the audience in your hand. It is hard to explain but it is all about capturing a moment. One song I really love to dance to is 'The Power Is Mine,' by the Lords of Acid."

I confessed I had never heard of the Lords of Acid, let alone this song, so I asked her for some of the lyrics.

"Oh, come on," she said. "You must know this song! 'The Power Is Mine' has such a great beat."

Leyla's upper body began to move to the music in her mind. She closed her eyes and for the first time that night I couldn't resist the temptation and let my gaze drop to the V-neck of her black fitted blouse. I looked at her breasts and then realized that, yes, beyond a doubt, the power was hers. Leyla began to sing. The lyrics were all about quenching hot desire, being filled up with fire and knowing it's never enough. The random lines that I managed to write down went something like this:

> *Come on boy obey me*
> *Come on boy obey me*
> *Lick my boots to please me . . .*
> *You are just a dog on a leash*
> *Lick me baby lick me*

The song ended with:

> *I can break your will—I can make you kneel*
> *I can force you to crawl and to lick my heels*
> *Cause the power is mine.*

"Quite an impressive ballad," I said when she was finished. We all laughed, but at the next table I thought a man might need the Heimlich maneuver to dislodge the food jammed in his windpipe by Leyla's words.

"All sorts of people came to Heart Breakers," Leyla continued. "Happiness and sadness, despair and joy, and all of the major issues of life walked through the doors every week. The club was a perfect microcosm of the world outside. We had our regulars, like Oliver, who we made friends with. Then we had the Dom [Pérignon] Guys. The ones who would pay the house about $200 to have one girl drink a glass of champagne with them at their table for ten or fifteen minutes. We identified other guys as one-timers. Let me give you a good example of a one-timer. I was working at the club on a slow afternoon. The place was virtually deserted and I was up onstage pretty much just dancing for myself to pass the time. No stripping, just dancing. After my set I was on my way to the restroom when a guy handed me a folded bill. I thought it was a ten but in the bathroom I discovered it was a $100 bill. This was unusual, so when I came back on the floor I went up to thank him. He just waved me away politely and said, 'We don't need to talk. I just want you to know I like how you dance.' Over the next two hours he ended up giving me another $500. He walked out the door and I never saw him again. We also had our fair share of business professionals and state politicians. These guys were usually respectful and they understood the exchange of services—money for female companionship and maybe a bit of innocent flirting. For them, it was not a sexual thing. And of course we had the religious wackos. I never bothered to try to figure out those guys."

"And what about the customers you didn't like?" I asked.

"It was a strange feeling to perform for people we despised, but these men, and a few women, were few and far between and of course when they showed up we were careful not to let our true feelings show. To do so would have been unprofessional. Instead, we just took their money with a smile. All of it, if possible. When they start asking around for the nearest ATM machine, you know you are doing a good job.

"And there was another thing going on. I'm not sure what the connection is, but many of the girls had been sexually abused as children and they carried a grudge. On the other side, we had our fair share of guys suffering from what we called the High School Prom Queen Reject Syndrome; the guys who got shot down by high school heartthrobs. They never got over it and they wanted to get even by being mean to the dancers. I can't tell you how many times I found girls crying in the back room because some jerk had hurt their feelings. And then you had the normal man/woman push/pull sexual attraction thing going on at the club. It is difficult to stay in this profession very long without developing a pretty low opinion of some men. To keep things in perspective it really helps to have a good sense of humor, and a finely honed appreciation for the absurd."

Oliver described how many of the dancers had a way of attracting psychotic boyfriends. It seemed to be an occupational hazard. The girls came from diverse walks of life, and many of them were registered nurses or worked as other sorts of caregivers. Kara had been a professional dancer with Carol Armitage in New York City for years before she became a stripper at Heart Breakers. Now she works as a financial adviser with Merrill Lynch. Tammy was a high school dropout, one of those people who never believed they could do anything. When she first came to the club she was streetwise and hard, a substance abuser with a violent boyfriend. The dancing softened her, made her more of a balanced person and calmed down her anger. She dumped her boyfriend, went back to school and became a pharmacist. Stephanie was a former bicycle messenger whom Oliver described as one-third babe, one-third biker chick and one-third rugby player. "Nobody messed with her," he said, "because she was a force to be reckoned with." She eventually went on to become a Sacramento firefighter. Oliver explained how he enjoyed the social interactions with the dancers more than anything else, especially talking to them about their lives.

"How much would a regular customer expect to spend tipping dancers?" I said.

"A good customer might spend $500 to $1000 on a big night," said Leyla. "But usually it was less than $200. I would guess $50 to $150 would be the average, but Oliver would probably have a better idea about this."

"One knucklehead customer burned through a $50,000 inheritance in a year," Oliver told us. "I seem to recall he had opposable thumbs, but I am not sure if he had a measurable IQ. No one on the softball team liked him and the girls thought he was a creep. But that didn't stop them from doing their job and helping the guy to blow his wad. He bragged that he could have any girl in the house, but it was a well-known fact that the girls wouldn't have touched him with a fork. After the money was gone he didn't come back to the club and nobody missed him or talked about him."

Oliver excused himself from the table to go use the men's room and while he was gone, the waitress brought our check. Without a word Leyla handed me her reading glasses when she noticed I was having trouble checking the bill in the dim light. After I paid, I looked up at Leyla who returned my stare. We sat at the table looking at each other for several seconds without speaking.

"Are you for real?" I said.

"What do you mean?" she replied.

"I can't help but feel you have been playing with me and treating me like a potential client. In a nice, charming, professional sort of way, mind you. How did you put it? By being the perfect reflection of the client's fantasy? So, tell me, what is my fantasy about you?"

Leyla smiled and said, "I honestly don't know. You will have to study the reflection and decide for yourself."

"OK, how about this?" I said. "You are a unique combination of intellect, charm, honesty, candor, humor, natural beauty and understated sexuality. You are a realist. You know the pathetic and dark side of people, but you live in hope."

Leyla laughed. "Much too flattering, but I can live with that," she said. "You have to understand that most of my time is now spent changing diapers and walking around the house in flannel pajamas with baby barf on my shoulder. The transition from conservative Catholic schoolgirl to stripper was easy compared to the emotional challenge of switching from being an object of intense desire to being a mom. But don't get me wrong, I love my little girl with every atom of my being."

"We just have a few minutes, before Oliver comes back, so I am wondering if you can tell me what it is that makes your friendship with him work. Or is it just your professional skill and knowledge of men that makes business-as-usual look and feel like friendship?"

"Business is business and I am very good at what I do. Sometimes money is involved, but the friendship is real. Oliver is an honest and good person. He is generous, not just with money, but with his concerns for people and with his emotions. I don't know if this comes from his gift for observing and studying birds and other wildlife, or whether it is the result of caring for his mother. Oliver is reliable, sweet, thoughtful and kind, but like a lot of other people he is also lonely and this makes him vulnerable. In the club, you have all sorts of men getting drunk and then making insulting or degrading comments. The girls don't think twice about taking advantage of these jerks. But Oliver never did that. He saw the dancers as human beings, as his friends, not as sexual objects to be ridiculed. I returned his friendship and respect by letting him into my private life. I allowed him to step over that line. Oliver listens to me when I need a sympathetic ear and I can talk to him about anything. He lets people be themselves. I trust him to be open and straightforward and to be a good friend, and that is something I can't say about most of the men I have known. If I could have one wish come true for Oliver, it would be for him to find a good woman to share his life."

Oliver returned to the table and as we stood up to leave our waitress came over to say good-bye. She gave Leyla an unexpected and spontaneous hug and, once again, I felt the people at nearby tables watching us closely. We walked out of the restaurant and then stood on the sidewalk for a few minutes, taking in the warm night air. Leyla shook my hand firmly and thanked me for dinner and the interesting conversation. She handed me a piece of paper with her home phone number and asked me to call if I had any other questions. Oliver told me he would make plans to take me out to the sewage ponds to observe the nesting shorebirds, and that there was a huge California Sycamore tree he wanted to show me at the northern end of the Yolo Bypass. Leyla gave Oliver a friendly hug and a light kiss on the cheek, and then the three of us turned and walked into the night in our different directions.

THREE NIGHTS ON THE MOUNTAIN

O N   A   R A I N Y   D A Y   in 1991 a Gulfstream II corporate jet, flying at 250 miles an hour, slammed into a wall of trees in the Borneo rain forest. On top of a mountain ridge, shrouded in rising mist, the wings and cockpit sheared off, followed by the tail section. The fuselage, with the twin engines still attached and running, cleared the ridge and continued to climb another 200 feet before starting its long free fall into a heavily forested valley. For nearly 450 yards the midsection of the fuselage remained airborne as it was transformed into a disintegrating rocket ship, hurtling out of control and leaving a trail of ragged, twisted metal, golf clubs, burst luggage, food trays, reading glasses, *Vanity Fair* magazines, body parts, and passengers still belted to their seats. In less than ten seconds, from the point of first impact, the shattered fuselage had roared its way to the bottom of a ravine where it crashed through the rain forest canopy and burst into smoldering fragments. Twelve people lay dead in the wreckage. But within moments, the natural sounds of dripping water, creaking tree branches, the soft patter of rain on leaves,

and bird and insect calls returned to the forest as if nothing
had happened.

From the top of the ridge to the farthest pieces of wreckage, the crash site covered more than a quarter of a mile of
trackless jungle covered with dense tropical vegetation. The
U.S. State Department and Malaysian authorities immediately
launched a massive search-and-rescue operation, but it took
two days for them to discover the small opening in the jungle
canopy which marked the spot where the plane disappeared
into the steamy shadow-world of the Borneo rain forest.

In all likelihood, I never would have heard about the
crash, but three months later a letter from Houston, Texas,
arrived at my apartment in Manhattan. It was sent from Roger
Parsons, whose wife, Annie, had died in the plane crash,
which occurred on a remote mountain in the Crocker Range
of Sabah, East Malaysia. The plane had been en route from
Narita, Japan, to Djakarta, Indonesia, as part of a business
trip organized by the U.S. oil company Conoco. In his letter,
Roger explained that he wanted me to help him visit the place
where his wife had died. They had been married three years
and she was only two weeks shy of her thirty-sixth birthday.
The letter described his intent to photograph and investigate
the crash site as evidence in eventual legal action. The bodies
of the twelve victims had been recovered by the Royal
Malaysian Air Force and the Criminal Investigation Division
of the Royal Malaysian Police about a week after the discovery of the crash site. Twenty-four numbered body bags of
human remains were brought to the Queen Elizabeth Hospital
morgue in Kota Kinabalu. Officials and legal representatives
from Conoco and Du Pont, the U.S. companies that operated

and owned the jet, immediately flew to Sabah to take control of the investigation. By the time the forensic work (commissioned by the two companies) started a few days later, only twenty-two body bags remained and there was no trace of either pilot. Roger wanted to know what happened to their bodies.

But Roger had another very specific and compelling reason why he wanted me to join him on the long journey to that distant mountain range overlooking the South China Sea. When Annie's body arrived in the United States her engagement ring was missing. Roger wanted me to help him search for the ring that he felt lay somewhere in the debris field of shattered vegetation, splintered tree trunks, human remains and fragments of twisted wreckage.

It seemed like an unusual request and I was fairly certain the ring would never be found because it probably had been taken by the search-and-rescue crew who first arrived at the crash site, or by members of the medical staff who worked at the Queen Elizabeth Hospital. The United States consul in Kuala Lumpur had already urged Roger to reconsider his plan because of the dangers of trying to land a helicopter in such a wild and remote jungle setting during the monsoon season. The U.S. Armed Forces Institute of Pathology forensic team leader, who never visited the site, Roger's employer and even his lawyer all advised him against going to the crash site. The National Transportation Safety Board investigator was the only U.S. government representative who had been to the site, and he encouraged Roger to go ahead with his plans. The consul said the journey, even if attempted under the very best of circumstances, would be extremely strenuous. He mentioned leeches, biting insects, poisonous snakes, steep cliffs, and the heart-stopping sense of panic and disorientation that can overwhelm a person unfamiliar with the limited views in the rain forest. The consul also made it clear that even if Roger managed to charter a helicopter and find a pilot willing to attempt a landing, he might be stranded on the mountain for days or weeks, waiting for a break in the weather so that the helicopter could return to pick him up. To further discourage Roger, the consul pointed out that an overland hike was out of the question because the plane crashed in an unexplored area far from any villages or roads, or even a jungle footpath. A walk to the site would require a guide conversant in both Malay and English. The person would have to be adept at long-distance Borneo jungle travel under the worst conditions. The guide must also be intimately familiar with the local tribal groups and their culture, and the consul could think of no such person.

It was at about this time that Roger Parsons walked into a secondhand bookstore in Dallas, Texas, where he experienced what he later described as a small miracle. Wandering the aisles, he picked up a copy of my book *Stranger in the Forest*, which is the account of my six-month-long, eight-hundred-mile crossing of the Borneo rain forest with groups of nomadic hunters and gatherers in 1982. In Roger's initial letter he mentioned that after reading my book he knew that I had the sort of experience and knowledge he was looking for. He went on to say that he felt I was "the chosen one." I was far less certain about how I might help him, but we began to discuss his plans.

When I suggested that he simply charter a helicopter to

visit the scene of the crash for a few hours and then fly out again, Roger told me he had already made up his mind that he wanted to stay at the crash site for several days and that I should join him. He wanted to leave as soon as possible even though the monsoon season might make it impossible to land a helicopter because of dense cloud cover and the turbulent afternoon winds and rainstorms that frequently sweep over the Crocker Range at that time of year. In the event a helicopter was unable to land, due to bad weather, Roger had a backup plan. He wanted me to help organize and lead an overland expedition to and from the crash site. I told him I would think about it. In the meanwhile, I asked him to send me the exact latitude and longitude where the plane went down, so that I could study my maps and get a better idea of what I might be getting myself into.

My initial feeling was that I didn't have the time to fly to Borneo to look for his wife's engagement ring. The other problem was that Roger seemed incapable of normal speech. His detailed descriptions of the crash, the probable causes that led up to it, and his stated objectives were so peppered with acronyms and obscure aviation terminology that I found his statements practically unintelligible. Listening to Roger's precise and controlled manner of speaking made me think that he was still in shock. Or he was so incredibly organized or so emotionally rigid that his world consisted entirely of facts and figures, problems and their numbered solutions—a far cry from the world I live in. But then I wondered if his obsessive behavior and self-restraint was possibly the only way he knew how to cope with the death of his wife. I asked him to send me a glossary of acronyms and their meanings, so that we could communicate more clearly. The list included things such as AWCs—Annotated Wreckage Components (located and identified pieces of the plane); CFIT—Controlled Flight Into Terrain (when a plane is flown into the ground intact); CVR—Cockpit Voice Recorder; NOTAMs—Notices to Airmen (frequently updated warnings and local information on airports around the world); AFIP—Armed Forces Institute of Pathology; GPWS—Ground Proximity Warning System (an onboard device to establish height above the ground, rather than above sea level); VOR—Very High Frequency Omnidirectional Range (a ground-based navigational aid to provide directional assistance to aircraft); TCA—Terminal Control Area (the controlled airspace surrounding airports); and ONCs—Operational Navigation Charts (detailed in-flight reference maps).

I became conversant in this strange nomenclature, but it was as if we were speaking a foreign language. At one point I asked Roger about the estimated speed at which the plane hit the trees and the general orientation of the crash site. He told me he had done some "rough calculations" which he would like to send me. A small sample of Roger's 137 pages of rough calculations regarding the last moments of flight before impact went something like this:

"Evaluating equation (EQ 34) at $t = t_2 + t_2 + t_1$ and using equation $v_1{}^*t_2 = d_2/\cos(i_1)$ to replace $v_1{}^*t_2$ with $d_2/\cos(i_1)$ in the second term on the right-hand side of equation $z = -g^*(t - t_1)_2/2 + v_1{}^*\sin(i_1)^*(t - t_1) + z_l$ yields: $z_2 - z_1 = -g^*t_22/2 + d_2{}^*\tan(i_1)$" ... and so on.

To give a sense of Roger's attention to detail, I should

probably mention that he had calculated the speed of the plane as it hit the trees to the ninth decimal place. But then, in a rare moment of clarity, Roger dropped the equations and acronym usage from our conversation long enough to explain that this would also be a sentimental journey. He wanted to visit the crash site in order to stand at the scene of his wife's death. He also planned to erect a small memorial plaque in her honor. Roger told me that on September 4, 1991, moments after the crash, he had woken up at 1:30 A.M. in Dallas. He felt his wife's presence, as if she was calling to him. When he told me these things his voice softened slightly. I was touched by his words and the sincerity in his voice, and at that moment I realized I no longer had a choice. Despite my work schedule, and whatever else was going on in my life, I knew I would join him on this strange journey to the other side of the world to look for his wife's engagement ring.

We set a departure date, made our plans, and I told him what clothing and equipment to bring. He sent me a plane ticket and six weeks later the two of us, along with his brother-in-law Kevin Cook and a local Kadazan man by the name of Ebit, were passengers in a helicopter flying low over the Borneo rain forest. Jostled by gusting winds and pelted by a torrential rainstorm, the pilot struggled to control his aircraft as we searched for a hole in the cloud cover. We were trying to locate and land in a tiny clearing high on the northeast spur of a mountain marked Peak 4818 on the map. The wild heaving and plunging motion of the helicopter was stomach-churning and at one point Kevin, who was a seasoned veteran of rough flying conditions in small helicopters, spoke into his headset and told us that if we needed to throw up we should place our mouths inside our shirts to contain the vomit and keep it from flying all over the cabin.

"As a courtesy to the pilot and your fellow passengers," he said.

The helicopter continued to circle and hover a few hundred feet above the forest canopy as a green sea of trees and rolling mist swirled beneath us. We caught occasional glimpses of giant tree crowns and steep mountainsides covered in primary rain forest, but we were unable to find the crash site because of limited visibility. With fuel running short and weather conditions deteriorating, we regained altitude and flew back to the airstrip at Kota Kinabalu to wait for a break in the weather.

We were grounded for several hours and during that time I thought about the events that led up to the crash. Weeks earlier, Roger had sent me a cassette tape of the cockpit voice recorder which covered the last thirty-two minutes of flight, including the sound of the wings hitting the wall of trees. In my office I had played the tape dozens of times, and it always left me with an eerie sensation of knowing that the two pilots and ten passengers were about to fly into a jungle-clad mountain and die violent deaths. Over and over again, I listened to the droning of the engines, the crackling static of the radio, and the steady voice of the air traffic controller at Kota Kinabalu Airport directing the takeoff and landing sequences for aircraft. The self-assured and easygoing Texas drawl of the pilot and copilot in the Gulfstream jet was easily distinguishable from the voices of the Australian, British and Malaysian pilots in the area. The good-natured and laconic comments coming from the Gulfstream jet gave no indication of impending danger until the last few minutes of flight, when the growing uncertainty of the pilot and copilot became apparent in their speech patterns.

The jet was well north of the Kota Kinabalu airport, at 31,500 feet, when the air traffic controller directed the pilots to decrease their speed and descend to 15,000 feet. When the jet arrived over the airport, the pilots were directed to descend to 9,500 feet and maintain a holding pattern south of the airport as a Malaysian Airlines commercial jet made its final approach for landing at Kota Kinabalu. Air traffic control directed the Gulfstream to continue its descent to 6,000 feet, on a heading of 210 degrees. Regardless of how many times I have listened to the tape, the last few minutes of conversation between the pilot and copilot and with the air traffic controller continue to haunt me.

"When do you want to start down?" said the copilot.

"Let's wait awhile," said the pilot. "If we're gonna have to hold, I'd rather stay up here and save the fuel. We should be on the ground at Kota in about fifteen minutes. Basically, we're out of fuel."

"Shall I call in [for fuel]?" said the copilot.

"No, I'll try and give 'em a call. You monitor the descent."

For the next several minutes their growing confusion and disorientation was reflected in a fragmented conversation consisting of a series of comments such as: "What do we do, just go to the VOR and get on that arc?" "Yeah, that's what I said." "What radial are you on?" "What? I didn't hear what he said" . . . "I didn't either" . . . "Affirmative? I still don't understand" . . . "Do we have to hold?" . . . "I don't know."

"Well, I GOTTA know," the pilot said sharply to the copilot.

Because of the confusion in the cockpit, the pilots did not descend over the airfield as directed by the air traffic controller. For unknown reasons the pilots did not slow the aircraft to approach speed when directed to do so and this error caused them to pass over the airport nearly fifteen minutes ahead of schedule and about 11,000 feet too high. By the time they were cleared for their approach on reaching 4,000 feet, the Gulfstream was much further south of the airport than the air traffic controller realized. They were also well below the mountaintops of the Croker Range that lay directly in front of them and only a few miles distant. The plane was equipped with both a barometric and a radar altimeter, which told the pilots how high they were above sea level and above ground level, but without a ground proximity warning system onboard, they had no instrumentation that sounded an alarm as the mountain slopes gradually came up to meet them. With visibility severely limited due to clouds, the plane miraculously flew through a low pass between two mountains. The Gulfstream cleared the mountain range and was headed south, into open air and safety, when the copilot spotted a forested mountain peak a few hundred yards to his left, at eye level.

"We're getting pretty close to the hills here," said the copilot.

"Well, yeah, I KNOW it," said the pilot. "I'm gonna turn to the right."

And as he did so, the pilot started to bring the plane around toward the west and back toward the mountains they had just escaped. The Gulfstream was now on a collision course with Peak 4818. More trees came into view beneath the plane.

"God . . . I'll tell you . . . ," the pilot seemed to say to himself. "I don' like what we've got," he continued after a pause. "I'm climbin' this sucker outta here."

The jet engines accelerated as the pilot pulled back on the control yoke in order to gain altitude, but not so abruptly as to alarm his passengers. The towering ridge line of trees was now less than 1,500 yards in front of the plane. In my mind's eye, I imagined the passengers quietly reading books, listening to music or engaged in casual conversation. They sat in air-conditioned comfort, sipping early morning coffee and writing postcards as they were lulled by the gentle vibration of a plane in flight. But as the plane approached the mountain the gusting wind and down drafts must have shaken the aircraft and alerted the passengers that something wasn't quite right. The pilots could not have known it at the time, because of the thick clouds, but if the aircraft had gained another fifty feet of altitude it would have cleared the trees. Seven seconds after the pilot's last words, the tape ended with the sound of a tremendous impact followed by the squelch of the cockpit voice recorder shutting off. With the cockpit torn away, the interior of the plane would have been instantly filled with a powerful blast of moist tropical heat. I couldn't help wondering how many passengers felt that sudden surge of warm, damp air or how many of them were still alive and conscious as the wingless fuselage soared high above the trees for nine long seconds, before the final plunge to earth.

On our second attempt to land at the crash site, we had

good visibility and the pilot managed to set the helicopter down despite a strong crosswind and the confined landing zone. We jumped to the ground and pulled our equipment from the helicopter. Following a drill we practiced before taking off, we all moved away from the aircraft, to a spot directly in front of the pilot so that he could see us, then gave him the "thumbs-up" sign that all doors and cargo hatches were shut and that everyone was clear of the tail rotor. Deafened by the sound of the roaring engine and buffeted by the powerful downdraft of the main rotors, we shielded our faces from flying debris and dust as the pilot lifted off. Within a few moments the helicopter was airborne and then it disappeared beyond the wall of trees. The terrific sound of the engine and the rotor blades beating the air faded. This noise was replaced by an unusual silence, occasionally interrupted by the sound of sheet-metal debris flapping in the wind as a warm wind rustled through the trees.

We stood on the northeast spur of Peak 4818. The immediate area was completely cleared of all trees. It had been the staging area for nearly forty people during the rescue operations, and this hilltop of destroyed forest would be our home for the next few days. The mountain was due north of the village of Melalap and due west of Keningau, two communities that I was familiar with from nearly twenty years of visiting Borneo. Further to the north, the undulating mountain range gradually fell away to hill country and then to the coastal plain. In the far distance, we could see the irregular coastline of the South China Sea.

Because of the uncertain weather, we had brought provisions for ten days and a battery-powered two-way radio for when we were ready to be picked up. We carried maps, a GPS, backpacks, and enough food and basic supplies to survive on in the event that we were forced to walk out. If we had to leave the mountain on foot, my plan was to head down the ravine, following the natural drainage from the final crash site, to a logging camp at the upper reaches of the Membakut River. This was a distance of less than ten miles in a straight line, but from previous jungle treks in Borneo, I knew it could take us several days, or longer, to cover that distance through the rain forest.

"Terrain clearance is a fundamental responsibility of all pilots," Roger said to no one in particular, as he surveyed the hilltop scene of devastation. It seemed a strange statement to make and no one responded to his comment.

Ebit was brought along because he took part in the original search-and-rescue effort. He was familiar with the layout of the crash site and he knew where most of the bodies and body parts had been found. We set up two separate camps on the only bits of flat ground we could find. Roger and Kevin erected a mountaineering tent near the helicopter landing site, while Ebit and I selected a site at the edge of the forest and set up a simple ridgepole with supports at either end. We covered this framework with a large ripstop nylon tarp and fastened the corners to nearby saplings with lengths of parachute cord. Our wide, open-air structure allowed for unobstructed, 360-degree views of the jungle and the clearing. The translucent, waterproof tarp protected us from the rain and when the sun was out it created a soft, diffuse light. We built stretcher-like cots off the ground and collected firewood for our cooking area. Once we were settled, the four of us headed southwest, following the telltale path of shattered tree trunks and pieces of wreckage.

Roger muttered something about vectors and radials, flight parameters and DME, but I had no idea what he was talking about and I didn't ask him to explain. Lost in a private world of pain and disbelief, Roger seemed remote and inaccessible as we surveyed the wreckage for the first time.

The trees at the first point of impact looked as if they had been sheared off by a giant weed-eater. The thirty-degree angle of splintered and broken trunks indicated that the plane was in a banked position when it plowed into the jungle. We stopped to inspect a mangled wing flap and the pedal assembly that once controlled the brakes. I suddenly caught the faint scent of putrefied flesh. It was not a constant smell, but came to me in isolated pockets of air, like undulating ribbons of scent that shifted with the breeze. The smell became more pronounced as an early afternoon wind blew up the ravine in our direction. I also became aware of the ominous sound of flies—unseen, but from the volume of the buzzing I knew they were still swarming on small fragments of mutilated human remains, three months after the crash.

"Bau daging busuk," Ebit said in Malay, as he noticed me sniffing the air.

"What did he say?" Roger asked.

"The stench of rotting meat," I said.

At the top of the ravine we came upon one of the pilots' caps and a few recognizable pieces of sheet metal from the wings. "AWCs—Annotated Wreckage Components," I thought to myself. Further down the slope, Ebit showed us the entire tail assembly, which was more or less intact. But most of the fragments from the plane were the size of dinner plates, or smaller. A deflated life raft hung high up in a tree. Tennis rackets, life vests, a Holy Bible, a pair of women's white cotton panties (Hanro of Switzerland), a tube of lipstick and other personal articles were strewn everywhere. Pieces of carpeting, snarls of multicolored wiring and fiberglass insulation littered the ground and hung from climbing woody vines. Nearly everywhere I looked I saw fragments of metal embedded like shrapnel in the tree trunks. Unopened beer and soft-drink cans lay scattered about the jungle floor as if left there as part of some macabre Easter egg hunt.

We spread out, but maintained voice contact with each other, as we continued to descend the steep slope. I picked up an aerosol can of Kraft Cheese Wiz. I was curious to know if Cheese Wiz could survive a plane crash, so I removed the cap and pressed the dispenser button. A steady stream of orange-colored processed cheese flowed smoothly from the spout. Ebit, who was standing next to me, wanted to know what the substance was. I told him it was food and then asked him to hold out his hand. I placed a toothpaste-length sample on the edge of his index finger and told him to take a taste. He put it in his mouth and considered the flavor and texture for a few moments before turning to one side and politely spitting it into the bushes.

"Thank you, but it is not what we Kadazan people know as food," he told me.

Further down the ravine I came upon a 35 mm Nikon camera. The lens was shattered, but when I tested the film rewind knob I realized, from the tension, that there was a roll of partially exposed film inside. I rerolled the film, opened the camera body, and put the film in my pocket.

"Roll of exposed film," I called out.

"Bag it," Roger yelled from somewhere in the distance.

I continued my steep descent into the jungle, searching through the debris. Visibility was limited to less than fifty feet, which was very disorienting, but it also made it easier to concentrate on nearby objects. I had never been to a crash site, and when I looked at the tiny pieces of metal scattered everywhere it was difficult to imagine that they had once been part of an airplane. We continued downhill by following a network of crude trails hacked from the vegetation, with jungle knives, by the search-and-rescue workers. A pair of panty hose fluttered listlessly in the trees like a double windsock, and I picked up a copy of *The Times Atlas of the World*. The cover was missing, but the pages were relatively undamaged apart from dampness and the binding was intact.

I found a mint-flavored condom in a foil wrapper. From where I stood, no piece of luggage or toiletry kit was visible nearby and this made me wonder where it had come from on the airplane. Was there a condom dispenser in the lavatory? Had one of the passengers been holding it in his or her hand at the moment of impact? In my mind's eye I imagined the plane exploding into pieces of flying metal and spewing its contents. In slow motion, I saw luggage ripped open and clothing flying through the air. In the shower of debris, the condom fell through the rain-forest canopy and, like a leaf, came to rest on the forest floor. I squeezed the wrapper and felt the lubricated condom slide beneath my fingertips. How ironic that its owner had died in the crash, but the condom had survived intact. Was it part of a tender joke between lovers or a husband and wife? And why mint-flavored? Were there other condoms in assorted flavors lying around the crash site? It seemed likely, and if so, what were the other flavors? Whatever plans had been made for the use of the condom had died with its owner. It made me think about who the condom belonged to. One of the men? One of the women? The pilot? The copilot? I had a pretty good idea of its intended use, but then I wondered if two of the people onboard were having an affair and what images might be found on the roll of film.

But regardless of where the condom came from, it made me consider the nature of life and love, and simple human pleasures, and how all of these things can be swept away in an instant. The moment before impact, the pilots and passengers breathed life. The plane was a graceful bit of machinery, defying gravity—soaring through the air one instant, a tangled mass of wreckage and mutilated bodies the next. In a sudden shock of realization the pilots must have seen the wall of trees directly in front of the plane, coming at them at 250 miles an hour. Too late to utter a word of warning, to catch their breath, or to cry out in fear. I briefly considered keeping the condom as a souvenir before I decided that I should leave it where I found it. The mint-flavored condom was someone else's story, and I decided to keep it that way. Unknowable, mysterious and private. I placed it on the ground and continued my search for the engagement ring.

I heard Roger call out that he had found two passenger

seats near a small stream. I worked my way down the slick, muddy slope by holding onto bushes and jungle vines until I joined him. A series of small waterfalls, hidden by the thick vegetation, made a soothing sound and the cascading spray filled the surrounding area with a gentle, cooling mist. The seats were remarkably intact, which made me wonder if the two passengers had remained belted to their seats during the wild, 450-yard-long, wingless plunge into the ravine.

"I think one of these seats was Annie's," Roger said. "According to a rough sketch map from the National Transportation Safety Board investigator, a young woman was found here." He looked from one seat to the next as if trying to determine which one was his wife's. He took video footage of the two seats for a few moments, and then, without a word, he went to stand by the stream. His back was turned to me, but I could see his body shake with emotion as he held the video camera at his side. It was an incredibly sad and tender moment. He had traveled halfway around the world to search for signs of his wife in this mess of airplane parts scattered through the rain forest. I imagined he was overwhelmed by dreams of her, and sweet thoughts, along with visions of her fear and pain and death. My instinct was to put my arm around him, but I thought better of it. Without a word, I walked back into the dense forest in order to let him be alone with his thoughts.

We filled our plastic water jugs from the stream and started the long, steep hike back up the ravine to prepare a simple dinner of steamed rice and tinned chicken curry. Roger and Kevin discussed how they would like to map out the crash site and search the area over the next few days. While we were boiling water for tea, Ebit described a body he found during his first visit to the mountain:

"It was a terrible thing. We saw a body slumped forward. It was a man and from a distance it looked like he was just sitting on the ground resting. But when we got closer, we saw the body was cut off at the waist. Legs gone. Head and arms also gone. It was just the upright torso—dressed in a white shirt. Hardly any blood, and so strange . . . because the necktie was still perfectly centered with the tie clip in place."

Roger and Kevin walked back to their tent and Ebit built up our fire for warmth against the chill night air on the mountain. We climbed onto our cots and within minutes I fell into an exhausted sleep beneath my blanket.

Sometime after midnight I felt Ebit shaking me violently.

"Wake up . . . WAKE UP! There is something out there, circling slowly!"

I listened briefly, but I didn't hear a sound. "Maybe an animal attracted by our food," I remember telling him in a half sleep. I rolled over, expecting to drift off again, but a few minutes later, Ebit let out a startled cry and shot bolt upright in his cot.

"Something touched me!"

I sat up, now fully awake, as Ebit continued talking. "Not an animal . . . it was something else. We Kadazan people call it *Penungu Gunung*—a mountain spirit. It walked around our camp and then tapped me on the head three times to wake me up and tell me the fire was out."

"Was this in a dream or did you see the spirit?" I said.

"Maybe in my dream or maybe I awake, but for local people like me there is no difference. It was a female spirit.

She had *kulit hitam manis* (literally, sweet black skin—a dark chocolate color), and she was dressed in a long white marriage gown with flowers around her head. She touched me."

Clearly, at this point, sleep was out of the question. We placed a few new branches on the glowing coals and rustled the fire back to life. Once the flames caught, we made a pot of tea and then stayed up for the rest of the night with our blankets wrapped around us while we talked about the crash and jungle spirits until dawn.

"My people do not call this mountain 4818, like on the map," Ebit said. "It has an old name, and we Kadazan people call it Bukit Marata. Like all mountaintops in our country, it is a place where the spirits live. Princess Boonyan is the spirit of Bukit Marata. She comes from where the rainbow starts and I think she the one who tap me on the head. After the crash, when no one can find the wreckage, the helicopter pilots believe that it was mountain spirit who call them, far away from original search area, to find the right place. But this is all local belief. The Kadazan people know this story, and some Chinese, but no one want to tell the American investigators and it is not mentioned in the official crash report."

Ebit asked me not to mention any of this to Roger or Kevin because he felt they would think of him as being a primitive person and a bad Christian. I told him I would keep all of this to myself. Shortly after sunrise, Ebit walked a short way into the jungle and left the first of several food offerings and gifts on a dinner plate for Princess Boonyan. These daily offerings consisted of a small amount of cold boiled rice with one or more of the following items: a few pieces of tinned pork or chicken, cigarettes, clear water in a cup or a chicken egg. When I told Ebit that animals would eat the offerings, he said that they would do so, but only after Princess Boonyan or other spirits had taken the essence of the things he left on the plate. He also cautioned me to ask permission of the spirits whenever I needed to urinate or defecate. "It is out of respect," he said. "We are human beings and we must do these things, but it is our custom to ask permission first."

After our breakfast, Ebit and I walked down to Roger and Kevin's camp. I didn't mention Ebit's story about Princess Boonyan, and that day we spent nearly eight hours in the ravine. I decided to begin a systematic search for the engagement ring by starting near the pair of seats that Roger located the previous day. I found a thin gold chain, fingernail clippers, a road map of Indiana, an appointment book, and personal letters—all of which I gave to Roger. We discovered one of the two Rolls-Royce engines about a hundred yards beyond the largest section of burned-out fuselage. The engine must have been running right up until the end because jungle vines clogged the intake cowling and trailed out the back of the engine. By midday the four of us were familiar enough with the terrain to wander on our own, up and down the steep slopes of the ravine. I found the top of a man's head, neatly cut off just above the hairline. The skin was intact, and the salt-and-pepper colored hair was still neatly parted on the side. High above me, and beyond reach, small bits of unrecognizable flesh hung like pieces of beef jerky from the trees. Roger and Kevin later collected these and other remains for DNA testing and identification back in the United States.

Our second night on the mountain, Ebit couldn't sleep. He was troubled by the mountain spirits. They were in his dreams and even when he was awake he felt their presence in the darkened jungle. He woke me up and we sat by the fire all night, drinking sweet black tea and talking about animism and how entering the rain forest is similar to the humbling and transporting experience of visiting a holy site, or standing in front of a great work of art. We both agreed that the mountain and the crash site felt like a sacred place.

The following morning at breakfast Roger mentioned that he had a strange dream just before dawn. "Well, I saw a woman. At first I thought it was Annie," Roger told us. Moments later Ebit nearly fell off his log as Roger described his vision of a woman with smooth dark skin. She was standing in the forest, in a long flowing white dress. It was nighttime, there was a garland of flowers around her head, and she was waving.

This revelation was too much for Ebit to keep silent about his identical vision from two nights earlier. He talked about his dream and then explained the meaning of *takaguran*, a local expression which refers to when a spirit speaks to you or makes its presence known. "When the spirit speaks, you must listen," Ebit said. "Sometimes there are no words, but you have to try to understand why the spirit has come to you. And whenever you enter the jungle you must do it like when you enter a house. These are not bad spirits, but they are powerful. They can do terrible things and we must treat them with respect. When the commando unit first arrive on the mountain, looking for survivors, they also ask for permission." Roger and Kevin listened to all of this with polite interest. Like me, they seemed slightly skeptical but they did not challenge what Ebit had said. Kevin merely responded by saying, "I'm cool with that."

On our third day in the ravine I found one of those plastic safety cards describing the correct position to take in your seat prior to an emergency landing. I looked at the familiar instructions about how to adjust the overhead oxygen mask and how to wear the personal flotation device. I continued to find small personal items: a woman's makeup bag, a Mont-Blanc fountain pen, a man's shaving brush, and a box of Band-Aids, but no engagement ring. Later that afternoon, Ebit and I unzipped the side pocket of a golf bag and found golf tees and about one dozen balls. The forest was littered with dozens of golf clubs in different sizes. I selected a #5 iron and Ebit picked up a #2 wood. We climbed to a fairly flat area in the dense forest and cleared enough of the surrounding vegetation so that we could swing the clubs. "Fore!" I called out, as I took my first swing. Beneath the rain-forest canopy, we took turns driving the shiny white balls into the jungle. A few of them hit nearby trees with a resounding "whack," but most of the balls simply disappeared as if they took flight and never landed. "A tough course," Ebit said. "I guess we won't need our putters." When we ran out of balls we laid down the clubs and continued our search for the ring.

During our third night on the mountain Roger told us more about his dream of the woman in the white flowing dress. In profile, she had looked like his wife, and the flowers of the garland were similar to the ones that Annie wore at their wedding. He described hearing the sound of cascading water. At first, he thought the sound was coming from a fountain in the cemetery where Annie was buried, but then he said that the sound was identical to the small waterfall near where he found her seat. For the first time since we arrived on the mountain, Roger seemed relaxed. I can't say that he had completely transformed himself from meticulous fact-finder and investigator to grief-stricken husband, but it was clear that these days and nights on the mountain had changed him. He talked about his wife and what she meant to him and about his sense of loss. I wanted to tell him that tears might help, but I didn't know him well enough and I decided to remain quiet. We never found the engagement ring, but on the last night before we left the mountain Roger showed us a few items that had belonged to his wife. A small carry-on travel bag, a ripped and partially burned halter top, and a plastic toothbrush container. Shortly after breakfast, on our last morning on the mountain, Roger and Kevin constructed a small wooden cross for Annie and planted it near the edge of the jungle clearing.

"In my language we call this *peringatan*," said Ebit. "A remembrance for Annie."

That morning, Ebit and I added a few scavenged items from the plane crash as part of our daily offering to Princess Boonyan: some Kiehl's eye cream, a tube of Lancôme mascara, a golf ball and tee, lip gloss, and a half-full, travel-size aerosol bottle of Chanel No. 19. Ebit arranged the contents on the dish and spoke the proper words of respect before we packed up our belongings in preparation to leave the mountain.

Ebit radioed the helicopter company and told them the weather was clear and that we were ready to be picked up. Within an hour, we spotted the helicopter flying in our direction. The pilot landed and the four of us climbed aboard. We fastened our shoulder harnesses and lifted off. The pilot made a series of slow figure-eight maneuvers over the crash site before heading back to the coast. During the first part of our return flight, no one spoke. Then I leaned forward from my seat behind Roger and placed my hand on his right shoulder. Without a word, Kevin and Ebit did the same on his left shoulder. Roger placed his hand on top of mine. The roaring sound of the engine made conversation impossible without our headsets on, but when he turned around to look at us his eyes were filled with tears and we could see him mouth the words "Thank you."

But that was not quite the end of the story. An hour later, in the lunchroom of the charter helicopter company, Ebit showed us a videotape taken right after the crash site was discovered. We saw the familiar landmarks of shattered trees, nearby mountains, and the larger pieces of wreckage. All of the rescue workers wore surgical masks and rubber gloves. The camera zoomed in on a label attached to a body bag. The handwritten letters were in English. They read: "Upper torso, right hand, pieces of leg." In the background I could hear the familiar buzzing sound of flies. The next image that came onto the screen was a severed human foot. A left foot from a woman. Everyone in the room seemed to take in a sudden gasp of breath as Roger asked Ebit to press the pause button. Roger stood up to take a closer look at the image frozen on the screen. After perhaps ten seconds of intense study he sat down and said, "It's not Annie's."

As the video came to an end, a different helicopter pilot walked into the lunchroom. By coincidence, this pilot was the

one who originally located the crash site. His name was
Amarjit Singh but everyone knew him as "The Cowboy"
because of his flamboyant personality and his highly skilled
style of flying. He talked about the search for the missing
plane. Based on the Gulfstream's last reported position, speed,
heading, and estimated altitude, rescue helicopters spent days
looking for the plane in the wrong place. At the end of one of
his search missions, Amarjit Singh decided to look further to
the northwest before returning to Kota Kinabalu airport. He
went silent for a moment before telling us that he felt drawn to
the area by an unknown force.

"I am a Sikh, and my religion does not believe in these
things, but I will tell you this: I felt myself pulled to the new
area. I don't know how to explain it. A voice or a power was
calling me to the north and west. I had enough fuel for a quick
look. I went there, and through a gap in the clouds I saw
something move in the forest. At first I thought it was a parachute caught in the forest canopy and blowing in the wind. I
circled and flew lower. I went into a steep banking maneuver
and for a moment I saw a woman below me. She was waving
to me. I radioed to base that I was at the scene of the crash and
that I could see a survivor. A young woman." The report of a
survivor was immediately sent to the United States consulate
in Kuala Lumpur, and from there calls went out to waiting
families in the United States. In Dallas, Roger was woken up
by a phone call in the middle of the night. He heard the news
and prayed that the survivor was Annie.

"And what did the woman look like?" Roger asked.

"Well, it was a strange sight," the Cowboy replied. "She
had dark brown skin—*hitam manis*, as we call it here." Ebit,

Roger, Kevin and I leaned forward in unison as the Cowboy continued his description. "She was dressed in a long flowing white robe or gown of some sort that billowed in the wind. She had a garland of flowers around her head and she was waving to me, beckoning me to come closer. The clouds obscured the view and I had to return for more fuel. But, before I left the area, I managed to get a positive fix on the location at 5° 22′ 30″ North, 115° 58′ 57″ West. It wasn't until the following day that the search-and-rescue people went in. But there were no survivors, I am sorry to say . . . and no trace of the woman in the white dress."

"What does it mean?" Roger asked Ebit.

"Princess Boonyan helped find your wife and bring her home. But beyond that, Roger, I do not know the meaning," Ebit said.

THE GHOST WIND

O N THE 2nd of July, 2000, the Indonesian tall ship *Dewa Ruci* sailed into San Francisco Bay with a huge skull-and-crossbones pirate flag flying from its mizzenmast. A marching band was on deck playing "Popeye the Sailor Man" and "Happy Birthday" in early celebration of Independence Day. High up in the rigging, dozens of cadets danced on the yardarms and waved to the tens of thousands of boaters and shoreline spectators who had come out to greet the *Dewa Ruci* and the rest of the fleet of tall ships from around the world.

Lines of rust and oil ran down the sides of the *Dewa Ruci*. Her sails were patched and stained with soot from long use, and it was clear that the ship had seen better days. By way of contrast, the pristine decks of the United States Coast Guard ship *Eagle* were lined with immaculate midshipmen standing motionless in their dress uniforms. But the visual highlight of the tall ship parade was the magnificent 391-foot-long, four-masted Japanese bark *Kaiwo Maru*. Set against a deep blue sky and the golden hills of the Marin headlands she sailed into the bay powered by a billowing cloud made up of 30,000 square feet of perfectly trimmed white sails.

By coincidence, I was rowing on the bay when the tall-ship fleet sailed through the Golden Gate. Attracted by the sounds of the marching band aboard the *Dewa Ruci*, I decided to follow the ship to where she berthed, just east of Fisherman's Wharf. I tied up the rowboat and went on board, where I met the ship's commanding officer, Commandant Darwanto. He was a handsome, compact man who reminded me of a slightly scaled-down Southeast Asian version of Dean Martin. We talked for about twenty minutes about Indonesia before he called for one of the cadets to take me on a tour of the ship. Belowdecks the companionways were filled with a pleasing combination of fragrances. The ones I could identify were those of clove cigarettes, enamel paint, clean engine oil, roasted coffee, steamed rice, freshly starched and ironed uniforms, and a pungent fermented prawn paste called *belachan*.

I was invited back for a buffet dinner that night put on by the Indonesian consulate. As I walked around the deck talking to the crew and the young cadets I kept hearing the word *lomba*, an Indonesian word that I was unfamiliar with. One of the cadets eventually explained that "lomba" means "race," and that in three days there was going to be a tall-ship race from San Francisco to Los Angeles. When I asked Commandant Darwanto if I could join him, he told me accommodations onboard were basic: cold-water showers, squat toilets, and Indonesian food. I explained that I loved Indonesian food and that I had lived in remote Indonesian villages, with primitive facilities, for months at a time. "Then please join us," he said. I told him I could sleep anywhere, even on deck, but he insisted that I stay in a crew member's vacant cabin.

Shortly after sunrise on July 5th, I stepped onto the creaking wooden gangway and went onboard with a small bag of clothes, camera equipment, and my foul-weather gear. The lines were cast off, the sails unfurled and with a fair wind blowing from the north, the 191-foot-long *Dewa Ruci* sailed beneath the Golden Gate Bridge far behind the main grouping of tall ships. At the ten-mile sea buoy the other ships turned south, but the *Dewa Ruci* held her westerly course and headed far out to sea, passing just south of the Farallon Islands. The sun set and the winds and seas continued to build in strength until by eleven P.M. we were heeled over and sailing at twelve knots with the bowsprit plunging into the waves and the port-side rail buried in the heaving seas.

In the wheelhouse, I studied the nautical chart and then checked the radar to locate the other tall ships that were starting to call in their positions to the race organizers. At around midnight, Commandant Darwanto and I fell into a conversation about the basic fact that Los Angeles lay to the south and we were still sailing west. I was curious to know why the *Dewa Ruci* was sailing at a right angle to our destination. He explained that the *Dewa Ruci* was no match for the other ships and that the only chance to make a respectable showing was by sailing far offshore in hopes of catching a more favorable wind. The week prior to the *Dewa Ruci*'s arrival in San Francisco, a storm had battered the ship and a heavy fog bank prevented her from sailing into the bay. At one point, they briefly considered sending out a distress call to the U.S. Coast Guard because of engine failure, but Commandant Darwanto felt that to continue under reduced sail and face the storm conditions was the best sort of training for the 150 young cadets onboard.

"The cadets will learn about high-tech communications and warfare on our modern battleships," said Commandant Darwanto. "But the purpose of the *Dewa Ruci* is to teach them seamanship, to be good-hearted and brave, and to face all challenges with hope."

During that terrifying week of storms, the ship sailed up and down the coast about fifty miles offshore. After nearly two months at sea since leaving Indonesia, they had nearly run out of water and food as the cadets battled to keep the ship in a position to enter the Golden Gate the moment there was a break in the weather. Those days of violent winds and heaving seas, torn sails, damaged gear and engine problems gave Commandant Darwanto and his crew ample opportunity to test themselves and to study the wind and sailing conditions off the California coast.

This is why, during the early hours of the race, while the rest of the fleet had set a direct course due south, closely following the coast from San Francisco to Los Angeles, the *Dewa Ruci* headed further out to sea in search of a wind that would bring her back to the coast at the finish line between Santa Catalina Island and Long Beach Harbor. This tactical move meant that the *Dewa Ruci* would sail a much longer distance than the rest of the ships.

The first night at sea, the thrilling motion of the ship and the excitement of being under full sail made it impossible for me to sleep. I spent hours talking to the helmsmen and standing on deck looking up at the stars and feeling the powerful gusts of wind that drove the ship through the waves and into the darkness. By two A.M., we were more than fifty miles off-shore when we altered course and turned south, hoping that the wind would hold. We were sailing at the ship's maximum speed, but the *Dewa Ruci* was in dead last, more than thirty miles behind the leading ships that had already passed Santa Cruz, headed due south.

Shortly after breakfast that morning, in the officers' small but cozy mess hall, Commandant Darwanto asked if anyone was interested in some karaoke practice. The officers sang songs such as "Oh! Carol" by Neil Sedaka and "Diana" by Paul Anka. But when it came to my turn, First Mate Agustus asked me to sing "Rawhide" in order for the officers to learn the proper cowboy accent. I went through the song twice and then Chief Deck Officer Irvansah belted out a credible version of his own with a slight Indonesian accent. Commandant Darwanto distinguished himself with an excellent version of "Are You Lonesome Tonight" by Elvis, and it was not until midmorning that we took a well-earned break from karaoke and ascended the narrow companionway steps to the wheel-house in order to check our progress. Four cadets were out on deck struggling with the six-foot-tall twin steering wheels in an effort to maintain control over the ship. By this time the *Kaiwo Maru* had a commanding lead, far down the coast and well on the way to her anticipated victory.

The *Dewa Ruci* was one of the oldest ships in the fleet and, beyond a doubt, she was in the worst possible condition. I never saw a lifeboat or life jackets onboard. Doors were falling off their hinges and a makeshift smokestack had

belched soot and unburned diesel fuel onto the gaff-rigged
mainsail on the mizzenmast. I loved the spirit of everyone
onboard, but I couldn't help thinking that we were like a mule
racing with thoroughbreds. Two days earlier, at the conclusion of a pre-race briefing with the other ship's officers, I
came away with the distinct impression that the *Dewa Ruci*
was considered to be little more than a nautical disaster waiting to happen. Most of the other ships in the fleet featured
state-of-the-art marine technology and sophisticated operat-
ing systems. They had access to satellite imagery and weather
fax printouts, with wind and wave analysis, to help them
anticipate any possible wind shift that could be used to their
advantage. By way of contrast, the *Dewa Ruci*'s autopilot was
broken, which meant that she had to be manually steered
twenty-four hours a day. The stained and tattered sails were
reefed, unfurled and trimmed by hand; navigation was determined by radar, sextant and dead reckoning. Weather pre-
dictions were made by looking at the sea and sky. Unless
something unforeseen happened, the consensus was that the
Kaiwo Maru would win the 380-mile-long race in approximately forty-five hours. *Kaiwo Maru*, in Japanese, means
"King of the Sea" and no ship expected to seriously challenge
her on the run to Los Angeles. That is, with the notable exception of the *Dewa Ruci*.

Once we had finally headed south, the winds continued to
pick up and at about four A.M. the topsail on the foremast blew
out. The popping sounds of the shredded canvas sail sounded
like the crack of a bullwhip, and in a heaving sea, with the ship
rolling wildly from side to side, it was a very dangerous time
to go aloft. The flapping sail could easily knock a man from

the yardarm and the one-hundred-foot fall to the deck would be fatal. If a cadet fell from a yardarm and into the sea at night under full sail there would be little chance of picking him up. All of the cadets were ready to climb the mast, but Commandant Darwanto knew his crew. He called for Cadet Wildan Ardiansyah, a tall, silent young man who played the big bass drum in the marching band dressed in a full-length, powder-blue walrus suit. The officers and cadets called Wildan Ardiansyah "Superman" because during the two-month-long voyage from Surabaya to San Francisco, he had proved himself to be the strongest and most fearless cadet aboard the *Dewa Ruci*.

A few minutes later, Cadet Ardiansyah appeared on deck, barefoot, with his climbing harness fastened to his body. He saluted Commandant Darwanto, and after a brief discussion, he leapt into the rigging and started to climb, quickly and confidently, into the darkness overhead. We couldn't see what he was doing, but no more than twenty minutes later he was back on deck with a flushed, wild look of excitement on his face. He quietly described in a few modest words how he had furled the remnants of the sail to the yardarm by himself. As he stood there in the faint light coming across the deck from the wheelhouse, it seemed as if he was vibrating with energy from his astonishing feat. It was decided that it was too dangerous to do anything more that night. The following morning other cadets would replace the damaged topsail.

The ship continued through rough seas at eleven to twelve knots with the wind gusting to thirty-five and forty knots. The *Dewa Ruci* rolled beneath us, bucking and heaving with the deck awash. I watched the bowsprit bury itself into the waves and then rear up high in the air, and this made me wonder what it must have been like for Cadet Ardiansyah at the top of the foremast swinging wildly from side to side. Each plunge of the bow was followed by a torrent of salt spray that pelted the deck as we pounded our way south beneath a canopy of stars. It was impossible for me not to be electrified by the powerful motion of the ship under these conditions and at first light I recalled John Masefield's poem "Sea Fever." Buffeted by the wind and swayed by the heaving and rolling motions of the ship, I remembered the first few stanzas:

> I must go down to the seas again,
>   to the lonely sea and the sky.
> And all I ask is a tall ship
>   and a star to steer her by;
> And the wheel's kick and the wind's song
>   and the white sail's shaking,
> And a gray mist on the sea's face
>   and a gray dawn breaking.

The wind held steady for the first two days, but by dawn on the following day the race leaders were becalmed somewhere off Point Conception, north of the Channel Islands. A whale breached not far from our starboard bow and I could feel the *Dewa Ruci* slowing down. The sun came out and as the sails fell limp we glided to a dead stop upon an undulating glassy blue sea. The ship rolled gently in the ocean swell and the wooden deck creaked in the midday heat, but apart from the gentle murmur of voices and the occasional slap of a sail or thump of a wooden block on the deck there was very little to intrude on the timeless scene of a tall ship becalmed at sea. Captain Darwanto looked aloft and said, "Layar-layar tidak mau makan angin [The sails don't want to eat the wind]." No other ships were in sight and as I leaned back against a giant coil of rope to contemplate the peaceful view before me, the deck speakers exploded with the music of "Sugar Pie, Honey Bunch" by the Four Tops. Throughout most of that afternoon everyone sat on deck listening to love songs like "Only You" by Roy Orbison and the joyous lyrics of "Dancing in the Street" by Martha and the Vandellas. Emmylou Harris singing "If I Could Only Win Your Love" put everyone into a trance. The cadets loved these songs. They would get up and dance spontaneously and the lyrics helped them to practice their English. For the officers, the music served another purpose by preparing them for the nightly karaoke competition after dinner.

At sunset a fresh breeze picked up, but the wind was from the south and it pushed us back toward San Francisco. Cadet Khalimul told me he didn't mind being becalmed because when the ship was not rolling and pitching, it was easier to play chess and Scrabble. The cadets passed the time by napping in the sun, doing sit-ups or making decorative rope patterns on the deck. In the wheelhouse, I listened to the marine band radio reports from the other ships. There was talk of canceling the race due to lack of wind and lack of time. The fleet was due in Long Beach Harbor for another waterfront parade in three days and for this reason several of the ships decided to drop out of the race and start their engines to cover the remaining distance. Tempers were wearing thin on the

Kaiwo Maru. The ship was built to the very highest standards and she was manned by an experienced crew that was accustomed to winning races under all weather conditions.

The more modern ships in the fleet had global positioning systems that determined their exact location within a few yards. To help train the cadets, the *Dewa Ruci* used a compass, radar, sextant, a sharpened pencil and a well-worn nautical chart, covered with smudged erasure marks, to establish the ship's position within a few miles. The brief, no-nonsense position reports from the U.S. Coast Guard ship *Eagle* set the standard for the usage of precise military jargon. Even simple comments on wind direction and speed displayed a daunting competence for all things nautical. I imagined these soulless, measured and perfectly modulated voices would sound exactly the same if they were directing a live naval battle. But hidden in these radio reports I detected a subtle but growing sense of frustration as the fleet entered its second day with no wind. *Kaiwo Maru* was dead in the water and drifting toward Santa Monica, approximately thirty miles north of the finish line.

But all was well aboard the *Dewa Ruci*. Chief Deck Officer Irvansah slipped on a pair of wraparound sunglasses with black frames and called all hands on deck for ballroom dance practice. "Officer and gentleman training," Commandant Darwanto explained to me. Dressed in their navy-blue jumpsuits, the cadets selected partners. Officer Irvansah climbed on top of a tall wooden crate with a microphone in hand to demonstrate the basic steps and turns of the cha-cha-cha. An electric keyboard player began a song and within minutes, the deck was alive with young cadets looking at their feet, and shuffling back and forth as they counted off their steps and practiced their moves. I turned to Commandant Darwanto, and nodded my head in approval.

"Wait until you see them polka," he said.

Country and western music was next, and Officer Irvansah demonstrated his version of Western Swing dancing. Once the cadets were in motion I turned to Commandant Darwanto and politely informed him the steps were not entirely correct. Commandant Darwanto walked up to the keyboard player, picked up the microphone and announced that a new *Tukang Berdansa Cowboy*—Master of the Cowboy Dance—would now give them a special lesson. I showed Officer Irvansah the basic steps and twirls without music. A Hank Williams song started to play and we danced for half a minute before selecting new partners. This pairing-off continued until all 150 cadets were dancing. At the end of the second song, I asked Officer Irvansah if he would like to teach them the Texas Two-Step. I explained how the two-step is danced to a four-count beat, but that only three counts are stepped. One, two, three/four—the third step being a quick two-step. It was easier to explain using the Indonesian numbers: *Satu, dua, tiga/empat.* We practiced the steps moving forward and backward so that we could demonstrate both the male and female parts. The music started up and the cadets were soon circling the deck, counting satu, dua, tiga/empat . . . satu, dua, tiga/empat while keeping time to the music. The scene looked like an all-male barn dance at sea. The Texas Two-Step was followed by a waltz and then a killer selection of polka's greatest accordion hits by Frankie Yankovic on his Solovox, Joey Miskulin, and finally Eddie Blazonczyk and the Versatones.

The cadets were winded from their dance practice, but when the polka music came to an end, Officer Irvansah decided to show them what he could do. He put MC Hammer's "Can't Touch This" on a portable tape player and as the music started he turned to me and said, "Hammer . . . he is a god." For the next few minutes he was in the groove as he danced himself into a frenzied state. Officer Irvansah burned up the deck. He cut loose with knee drops, shoulder spins and the splits. He could sing, strut, dance and get down with a vengeance. The cadets worshipped him.

Following ballroom dance practice, it was time for the midday call to prayer. Instead of playing a prerecorded tape, a man from the engine room came on deck to call out the proper Arabic words in a haunting, soulful voice as the Muslim cadets knelt down and conducted their prayer ritual.

After lunch, Cadet Heru Kristiono took me aside to explain the different parts of the ship. The masts were named after three famous brothers from the 2,500-year-old Hindu epic, the *Mahabharata*.

"The foremast is called Bima," Heru said. "Very brave. Big, strong and tough. He fight evil. Like Rambo. You see the mast has five yardarms. He is the strongest of the three brothers. The midmast, Arjuna, is very clever. He is tallest and most handsome. A playboy with many wives," Heru whispered to me. "We call the mizzenmast Yudistira. He is oldest brother. A good leader. Patient, kind and wise. He never get angry and he control Bima and Arjuna. He is at the back of the ship so he can keep his eyes on his two younger brothers. All three brothers are what we call Satriya warriors. Fearless, brave and with high moral standard. We cadets try to be like this."

"Who is Dewa Ruci?" I said.

"That is complicated story," Heru replied. "But at one point in the *Mahabharata*, Bima, the fighter, goes searching for self-knowledge. Not like Rambo, he want to improve his mind. But Bima fall into the sea wearing his armor and sink to the bottom. He marry the daughter of the sea-serpent king and then he meet Dewa Ruci who was very small underwater sea god. He has small size but big power equal to Bima. He also have the knowledge Bima looking for. So Dewa Ruci climb into Bima's ear and he stay there. In a way he become Bima's conscience and this is how Bima become more patient and wise."

On the other ships, I imagined strategy sessions and hours spent poring over incoming satellite weather reports in search of favorable wind patterns to help them win the race. That night, on board the *Dewa Ruci*, Captain Darwanto was also in a serious state of mind as he focused his thoughts and prepared for the last round of karaoke competition in the officers' lounge. With separate microphones held in their hands, First Mate Agustus and Commandant Darwanto fell silent as they readied themselves for their final songs.

"Crank it!" Commandant Darwanto finally called out. He cleared his throat, took a sip of water and launched into a beautiful rendition of "The End of the World" in a rich baritone. First Mate Agustus was visibly shaken by Commandant Darwanto's flawless performance but he managed to compose himself sufficiently to deliver an excellent version of Andrew

Lloyd Webber's "Any Dream Will Do." The song ended, accompanied by generous applause, but clearly Commandant Darwanto had now extended his unbroken karaoke winning streak to nearly three months. Up on deck, I could hear the faint sounds of a trumpet player practicing "The Star-Spangled Banner."

At 4:20 P.M. on our third day at sea the wind speed remained at two knots, which was not enough to get the ship moving. Sidiq, the chief navigation officer, finally picked up a conch shell and started blowing it at the wind speed indicator. The droning sound of the conch shell was intended to summon Dewa Bayu, the god of fair winds. Five minutes later the wind speed increased by half a knot. Officer Irvansah pulled a larger conch shell out of a drawer. He attached a trumpet mouthpiece to one end of the shell and started blowing it into a microphone that broadcast the haunting, mournful sound from the deck speakers. Dewa Bayu must have heard the call because within half an hour the dial on the wind speed indicator pointed at 3.25 knots, which was enough to get the *Dewa Ruci* moving. Over the next few hours a mysterious offshore wind, favoring our isolated position, far from the rest of the fleet, appeared from nowhere. The sails ruffled and then gently filled with air and the *Dewa Ruci* began to silently cut through the water. "Angin Hantu," Officer Sidiq told me, "the Ghost Wind."

The wind increased, the ship heeled slightly and before long we were sailing at eight knots on a course east southeast, headed directly for Catalina Island. The rest of the fleet was becalmed somewhere to the east, off the coast near Oxnard. A few more of the big ships dropped out of the race, citing lack of time and lack of wind. Late that afternoon we received a radio report that the *Kaiwo Maru* was still twenty miles short of the finish line. The King of the Sea had drifted into the busy coastal shipping lane, within eight miles of shore. The crew in the *Dewa Ruci*'s wheelhouse took turns blowing the conch shells throughout the night. No one could sleep because of the growing sense of tension and excitement and most of us were milling about the deck when at 1:30 A.M. a report came over the intercom:

"Speed: ten knots. *Dewa Ruci* closing on *Kaiwo Maru*."

At this point, Commandant Darwanto decided to pull out all stops. He turned off the karaoke machine halfway through a practice run of "Rhinestone Cowboy" and climbed into the wheelhouse to take command of his ship. All hands were called on deck to sing a Javanese folk song that is used by little boys when they need more wind to fly their kites. The song was called "Lagu Lil Ilir." Officer Irvansah translated the lyrics for me and explained that the song was about a simple cowherd who went searching for a young princess who became lost in the forest while looking for star fruit. I asked him what the song had to do with kite flying, or the wind, or winning tall-ship races off the coast of California. "This song comes from Central Java," he said. "It is a lesson about the importance of trying and never giving up."

In the predawn hours the *Dewa Ruci* moved into the lead. Offshore weather conditions held steady, and long before first light the *Dewa Ruci* was on a beam reach, with sails trimmed, riding the Ghost Wind toward the finish line. At 4:59 A.M., the *Hawaiian Chieftain*, a reproduction of an eighteenth-century warship, pulled alongside us. Hours earlier they had dropped out of the race and motored to our position to cheer us on. Three miles from the finish line they fired a deafening blast from a deck cannon and then turned their loudspeakers in our direction. The acrid cloud of black smoke still hung in the air as Aretha Franklin's "Chain of Fools" started booming across the water. From bow to stern and up in the rigging, the crew on the *Hawaiian Chieftain* started dancing, clapping their hands and singing to the music. The *Dewa Ruci* marching band assembled on deck to play "Popeye the Sailor Man" and at that moment I realized that unless we lost a mast, hit a submerged rock, were abducted by aliens, or the ship was struck by a meteorite and sank, the *Dewa Ruci* was headed for victory.

A few minutes later, just at sunrise, a group of cadets started shouting "Lumba-lumba! Lumba-lumba!" They pointed off the port and starboard bows to where more than a hundred dolphins were leaping into the air, leading us toward the finish line. Our deck speakers crackled to life with Marvin Gaye and Kim Weston singing "It Takes Two" and I asked myself, "Who made this movie?"

An announcement came over the intercom in a clear, steady voice:

"Seribu meter lagi." One thousand meters to go.

At 6:38 A.M. the *Dewa Ruci* rounded the northern end of Catalina Island and slipped across the finish line. Pandemonium broke out on deck. The marching band played John Philip Sousa's "The Stars and Stripes Forever," continuous cannon fire erupted from the deck of the *Hawaiian Chieftain*, and the drone of conch shells, trumpets and wild cheering from the cadets filled the morning air as the first orange rays of sunlight broke through scattered clouds and illuminated the lines of rigging and sails. Cadet Ardiansyah, dressed in his blue walrus costume, with the huge tusks, leapt about the deck beating insanely on his big bass drum. People were laughing with tears of joy in their eyes, blowing whistles, singing words of thanks to the god of fair winds, giving praise to Allah, hugging each other and dancing the polka.

"The Ghost Wind," Commandant Darwanto said, smiling to himself, as he stood in the wheelhouse surveying the scene of jubilation on deck. I reached into my shoulder bag for a warm bottle of champagne and we stepped into the early morning light to pop the cork and dance with the walrus.

Acknowledgments

I would like to thank Shelley Washburn, friend and farthest star, for editorial comments and suggested changes to the numerous versions of these chapters over the course of several years. For helpful insights and comments on chapters in progress or on the final manuscript: Ernie McCormick, Elaine Smith, Ken Eastman, Donna Allman, Stephanie Dowrick, Alice Erb, my sister Kennedy Hansen, Gordy Slack, Laurie Greig, Heidi Hopkins and David Hamilton.

At Pantheon Books: Dan Frank, for bringing me to Pantheon three books ago, and keeping me there. To my editor Edward Kastenmeier, editorial assistant Leah Heifferon, and especially art director Archie Ferguson for his discerning eye and quirky sense of humor when it came time to select a photo for the book cover. Janice Goldklang, publisher of Pantheon, for coming up with an inspired choice of book title. Copy editor Robert Hemenway, for his unbelievably thoughtful and thorough reading of the manuscript. All authors should be so fortunate.

This book would not have been possible without the help of many people. To mention only a few: Phillipe, Elvira and Valerie Braunschweig for introducing me to Arlette, Madame Zoya, Maurice Béjart, Sylvie Guillem, Michael Avedon and to the world of ballet in Lausanne, Switzerland and New York City. Gregory and Vladimir Manuel, who as children listened to several of these chapters when told in their original versions as bedtime stories. My fellow crew members and survivors of Cyclone Tracy on the Australian prawn trawler *Cape Bedford*. Alfie and Ella Mills of Thursday Island, Australia. Ralph Nona and his extended family of Badu Island, Torres Strait, Australia. Chief Tom Numake from the island of Tanna, Vanuatu, and his friend and partner in crime Chief Samson Kasso—the undisputed kava king of Middle Bush village. The late Don Tutu, who brought me back to life and then shared with me his vast knowledge of "night fishing" on the island of Male, Republic of Maldives.

At Mother Teresa's Home for Dying Destitutes in Calcutta: the late Mother Teresa, Sister Luke, my coworker and long-lost friend Jacqueline, and the Sisters and Brothers of Charity who continue Mother Teresa's work at the Kalighat Clinic.

Madame Zoya in New York City. Steve Chainey for introducing me to the Bird Man of Yolo County. Christine Deibel for an unexpected friendship and for lessons about courage, grace, and hope. Ornithologist, male model and banana-slug-sex fact checker Edward Whisler. Roger Parsons for drawing me into the circumstances surrounding the crash of Flight N204C in the Borneo rain forest that resulted in the tragic death of his wife, Ann. William Langewiesche for his illuminating and thoughtful comments on pilot error, plane crash investigations and obscure aviation technology. Commandant Darwanto, Chief Deck Officer and onboard dance instructor Irvansa, Iwan "Engine Room," and the cadets and crew members of the unsinkable Indonesian tall ship *Dewa Ruci*.

And finally, to a brave little girl named Zoe. A huge inspiration in a very small package.